A
BONNIE
SCOTTISH
COOKBOOK

Other
Books
by
Author

PASTA: PLAIN AND FANCY
THE MAGIC OF MUSHROOM COOKERY
YOGURT COOKERY
THE EASTERN EUROPEAN COOKBOOK
SOUPS & STEWS: ONE-DISH MEALS
THE BEST OF WESTERN EUROPEAN
COOKERY
THE DELECTABLE VEGETABLE
THE COMPLETE INTERNATIONAL SALAD
BOOK
THE COMPLETE INTERNATIONAL ONE-
DISH MEAL COOKBOOK
MEDITERRANEAN COOKING FOR EVERY-
ONE
THE COMPLETE INTERNATIONAL SOUP
COOKBOOK
THE COMPLETE INTERNATIONAL
BREAKFAST AND BRUNCH COOKBOOK

KAY SHAW NELSON

A BONNIE SCOTTISH COOKBOOK

EPM
PUBLICATIONS. INC.

1003 Turkey Run Road
McLean, Virginia 22101

Library of Congress Cataloging-in-Publication Data

Nelson, Kay Shaw.
  A bonnie Scottish cookbook / Kay Shaw Nelson.
    p.   cm.
  Includes index.
  ISBN 0-939009-25-0
  1. Cookery, Scottish.   I. Title.
TX717.3.N45 1989
641.59411—dc20   89-7778
                           CIP

EPM Publications, Inc.,
1003 Turkey Run Road
McLean, Virginia 22101

Printed in the United States of America

Cover design was adapted from the Shaw family tartan by Tom Huestis

Contents

To
the
memory
of

my Scottish parents,

DOLINA MACASKILL *and* ANGUS SHAW,

and
to
my daughter,

RAE KATHERINE NELSON

About the Scots, their Cooking and Oat Cuisine

It's about time to hoist "a cup o'kindness" and sing the praises of "guid Scottish fare."

Gather round ye Scotsmen wherever you are. Don your kilts, tam o'shanters, tartans and tweeds. Let's celebrate with the skirl of bagpipes, the burr of Gaelic balladeers, and the immortal poetry of Robbie Burns. And then, for old-times' sake, bid farewell with a "wee deoch-an-dorris," or drink at the door.

There have long been too many tedious jokes and errant legends about Scottish cookery. One of them is that Scots dine frugally on mundane fare, and we've all heard the ridicule about the curious and famous dish called haggis.

For gastronomes and historians as well as Scots themselves, I have written this book to set the record straight about the creative and nutritious Scottish cookery, including the cuisine of oats. The repertoire of traditional Scottish dishes, prepared and loved for generations, is both fun to cook and to eat.

This book reaffirms the Scots' keen sense of humor. Who but Scottish cooks would have created fare called Clootie Dumplin', Fatty Cuties, Fitless Cock, Hattit Kit, Howtowdie, Inky Pinky, Roastit Bubbly-Jock, Rumbledethumps, Tuppeny Struggles, Tweed Kettle, Wet Devil and Whim Wham, and such drinks as Whipkull, Het Pint and Auld Man's Milk?

Think of how many famous delicacies have been created by canny Scots—Arbroath smokies, black bun, butterscotch, cock-a-leekie, Drambuie, Dundee cake and orange marmalade, Finnan haddie, heather honey, kippers, oatcakes, scones, shortbread, smoked salmon, and Scotch broth, whisky and woodcock, to say nothing of the incredible haggis.

Early Scots enjoyed nourishing, straightforward fare that evolved over the centuries from a thrifty, wholesome diet into an inviting cuisine with sophisticated overtones. Long years of association with France during the Auld Alliance added many refinements to the basic dishes. Scottish cooking, goes the saying, is a "pastoral one that went to Paris and took on French airs."

Scots have a certain mystique about them that is not easily discernible. So does their cooking. It's much better than its reputation and is more versatile than is generally realized. The Scottish cuisine is distinct and inviting and can stand comparison with any other.

Scots "over the seas" or "far flung" have carried proudly their homeland clan, tartan, music and cookery traditions to the far corners of the earth. All it takes for a nostalgic get-together is a homey Scottish dish or two and a couple of Scots who can hoist a glass of whisky to start the singing of "Annie Laurie," "Comin' Thro' the Rye" and "Loch Lomond."

Scots everywhere are noted for their warm hospitality and sharing of food. At home and abroad they love the conviviality of lively annual festivals called Highland Games and Gathering of Scottish Clans (with athletic and music competitions, Highland dances, bagpipers, whisky tastings and the eating of Scottish food), as well as cherished holiday celebrations that honor ancient spirited traditions with joyous dining and drinking and are interspersed with exuberant toasting, orations, melodies and dancing.

It was my mother who originally aroused my interest in Scottish cooking. From her I learned about the delight and goodness of homemade soups, nutty-flavored oatmeal porridge, delicious scones eaten hot off the griddle, and buttery shortbreads.

When I was a child in Lebanon, New Hampshire, our family stories generally centered on one remote locale, the small isle of Cape Breton, just off the Nova Scotian mainland. For this was the beloved homeland of my Scottish parents and their forebears, the Morrisons, MacLeods, MacAskills and Shaws, who had settled happily in the inviting coves and impressive highlands to fish, raise sheep, spin, weave, knit and perpetuate their Scottish culture.

Such were the superlatives of the island's attractions that I was somewhat skeptical about the real enchantment of "Canada's Scotland." I particularly remember sitting in wide-eyed awe to hear about a real live giant in the family tree.

Years later while visiting in Cape Breton I learned that the reminiscences of my mother about our legendary cousin, the "giant," were indeed true. For in the small fishing village of Saint Ann's I went to the Giant MacAskill–Highland Pioneers Museum, dedicated to the memory of the seven-foot, nine-inch, 450-pound Angus MacAskill, once the "strongest man on earth."

There are many stories about his strength and Bunyanesque feats. Word of his deeds reached P.T. Barnum, who took Angus on tour for five years in the mid 1800s, billing him with Tom Thumb as the world's largest and smallest human beings. At the end of each act, Tom Thumb danced a jig on the palm of the giant's great hand. He visited Queen Victoria in London because she, so small, wanted to meet the largest man in her empire.

I was curious about his early life and diet. All I could learn was that it had been normal, nothing unusual. He did, however, eat a large bowl of crowdie (oatmeal and cream) after each meal, his admirers told me. Just another "braw Scotch laddie" brought up on a Cape Breton diet of parritch, bannocks and oatcakes, one of them told me.

Later in Scotland and in locales around the world where I met Scots, I would hear more about the virtues of tasty treats made with oatmeal. As you will see in this book, oats play an important role in the Scottish cuisine. Strangely, Americans are just now discovering the versatility and appeal of this humble food, something the Scots have known for centuries.

In early times oats became the primary source of sustenance for the Scots, for the hearty grain flourished in Scotland's cool northern climate. Through necessity, crofters' (farmers') wives experimented with using oats in their everyday fare and created the most practical and imaginative of all the world's oat dishes. An old Scottish cookbook stated quite correctly that the oat is "one of the sweetest grains to cook with."

Oats have a sweet, nutty flavor and crunchy texture and are an economical cooking and baking ingredient. Scots enjoy oats in soups, vegetable and meat dishes, seafood specialties, puddings, desserts, a wide range of baked goods, and drinks, as well as the traditional porridge and haggis. Their versatility shows throughout this book; there are twenty-five recipes for favorite Scottish oat dishes and drinks as well as descriptions of traditional oat specialties beginning on page 121.

Oats contain seven B vitamins and vitamin E. They supply nine minerals: iron, calcium, phosphorus, magnesium, sodium, potassium, copper, manganese and zinc. Oats have the highest level of protein of any grain and among the highest levels of thiamine and iron. Oats are naturally low in sodium, sugar and cholesterol.

Oat bran, the outer covering of the grain, is touted as the miracle food of the 80s by many health professionals. It is rich in water-soluble fiber that is believed to be helpful in lowering cholesterol levels for many persons when used as a part of a total dietary program. It has even been claimed to be the best of aphrodisiacs.

The canny Scots were years ahead of us in enjoying the best of food for the best of health. But the "flower of Scottish soil" is now ours to treasure and enhance the body and spirit. This book presents both traditional and modern Scottish culinary specialties ranging from wholesome, nutritious dishes to ambrosial sweets and tempting baked goods that Scots enjoy so very much. They also relish the rich dairy products, fruits and other grains used in making their luxurious desserts and tea-time fare.

I hope my book not only enhances your knowledge of Scottish cooking but adds variety and interest to your menu and brightens the dining experiences of everyone who sits at your table. As they say in Scotland for good luck, "Lang may yer lum reek." Long may your chimney smoke!

Starters

Scots enjoy delectable appetizers with drinks before dining or as an introduction to a meal on special occasions. Outstanding starters are seafood delights ranging from fresh oysters and poached shrimp to rich smooth smoked fish mousses. Other favorites include fish in a tassie (glass dish), game skree (a flavorful forcemeat), speckled dark green plovers' eggs, grouse pâté, coddled eggs with salmon roe, and iced melon with candied ginger and brown sugar.

Some of the piquant starters with amusing names were once called savories. The dishes were served as a separate course at the end of a meal to clear the palate after dessert in preparation for port and liqueurs. Today they are enjoyed as snacks, for luncheon or high tea.

Smoked Salmon

Scots are very fond of smoked fish (haddock, mackerel, herring, trout), which they relish in many dishes and enjoy as starters. The most luxurious and highly prized is their smoked salmon, an unparalleled delicacy. The quality of the North Atlantic fish and the superior cold smoking technique result in a distinguished flesh. Genuine smoked Scotch salmon is rich and succulent with a distinctly pleasing smoky flavor. It has a reddish-orange color and firm, very lean texture with a glossy sheen.

Slicing the salmon is very important. At a fish shop or seafood center, have the salmon cut in serving portions when you buy it and as close to serving time as possible. Purchase only as much as will be used because it does not improve with age and, once cut, begins to dry out. Serve cold.

If slicing a whole side of salmon at home, place the cold fish on a chilled marble slab. Slice on the diagonal or downward and outward with a long, very thin, flexible, sharp knife.

Most Scots prefer the salmon *au naturel,* without accompaniments. Serve each person a few large, thin slices with a wedge of lemon, a grind or two of pepper, and thinly sliced buttered or plain brown bread. Or the salmon can be served with a fresh horse-radish—whipped cream sauce or a garnish of sour cream and chopped fresh dill.

Kipper Pâté

This well-flavored spread is made with canned kippers, herrings that have been split, lightly salted and then smoked.

Makes 1½ cups

> 2 cans (3¼ ounces each) kipper fillets, drained, cut up
>
> ½ cup (1 stick) butter, softened, cut in small pieces
>
> 2 tablespoons fresh lemon juice
>
> 2 teaspoons minced onion
>
> 2 teaspoons Dijon-style mustard
>
> ⅛ teaspoon freshly ground pepper

Purée kippers, butter, lemon juice, onion, mustard and pepper in an electric blender or food processor. Spoon mixture into an earthenware or glass container. Leave at room temperature 30 minutes. Cover with plastic wrap. Refrigerate several hours, up to 2 days. Serve with thin slices of brown bread or toast.

Scots Toast

A long-time popular savory, Scots Toast was traditionally made of creamed fish on buttered toast. This modern version features mushrooms. It makes an appealing first course for luncheon or dinner.

Serves 4

> ½ pound mushrooms
> 2 tablespoons butter
> 2 tablespoons heavy cream
> ⅛ teaspoon freshly grated nutmeg
> Freshly ground pepper to taste
> 4 slices hot buttered toast
> 4 teaspoons anchovy paste
> 4 teaspoons finely chopped fresh parsley

Wash and dry mushrooms; slice thinly. Melt butter in a medium skillet; add mushrooms; sauté about 3 minutes, until just tender. Add cream and nutmeg. Season with pepper. Cook slowly 1 or 2 minutes.

Spread each slice of toast with 1 teaspoon anchovy paste. Arrange on individual plates. Spoon an equal portion of mushroom mixture over each slice of toast. Sprinkle each with 1 teaspoon parsley. Serve at once.

Ha' Pennies

These crisp Cheddar cheese rounds are a specialty at the annual Christmas Walk, a glorious Scottish celebration in Alexandria, Virginia.

Makes about 4 dozen

> 1 cup all-purpose flour
> 1/8 teaspoon cayenne pepper
> 1/4 teaspoon salt
> 1/2 cup (1 stick) butter, cool and diced
> 2 cups finely shredded Cheddar cheese
> 4 to 6 teaspoons light cream

Combine flour, cayenne and salt in a large bowl. With a pastry blender, cut in butter until mixture is like fine crumbs. Stir in cheese. Add cream, 1 teaspoon at a time, using enough to make a stiff dough. Gather into a ball.

Put on a flat surface. Cut into 2 parts. Shape each part into a long roll about 1 inch in diameter. Wrap each roll in plastic wrap. Refrigerate about 2 hours. Put on a flat surface. With a floured sharp knife, cut each roll into 1/4-inch slices. Place on ungreased baking sheets, about 1 inch apart. Bake in a preheated 375° oven about 12 minutes, until tender and golden. With a spatula, transfer to wire racks. Cool. Store in airtight containers.

Potted Shrimp

Scots are fond of pastes made with cooked meat or fish that are sealed in small pots to preserve them. Potted shrimp was once a favorite breakfast dish. Now it is traditional fare for afternoon tea and is a good appetizer.

Serves 6

>*1 pound tiny shrimp, shelled, cooked and deveined*
>
>*1 cup (2 sticks) unsalted butter*
>
>*⅛ teaspoon freshly grated nutmeg*
>
>*⅛ teaspoon cayenne pepper*
>
>*Freshly ground white pepper to taste*
>
>*6 watercress leaves or parsley sprigs*

Cut shrimp into bits. Combine 1 stick butter (cubed), nutmeg and cayenne in a medium saucepan. Season with white pepper. Heat slowly until butter melts and is foamy. Stir in shrimp; heat gently until coated with butter. Spoon mixture into 6 small pots, dividing equally.

Put remaining 1 stick butter (cubed) in saucepan; melt. Pour over shrimp to form a thin layer, dividing equally. Allow to set at room temperature. Cover each with plastic wrap. Refrigerate several hours, up to 4 days. Leave at room temperature about 1 hour before serving. Garnish each pot with a leaf of watercress or parsley. Serve with thin slices of brown bread.

Scotch Eggs

Fried sausage-covered boiled eggs, a favorite pub and picnic fare in Scotland, do well as appetizers.

Makes 6 whole or 12 halves

> 6 hard-cooked eggs
> Flour for dredging
> 1 pound bulk pork sausage
> 2 tablespoons minced onions
> 2 tablespoons chopped fresh parsley
> Salt, pepper to taste
> 2 eggs, beaten
> Fine dry bread crumbs
> Vegetable oil for deep-frying

Shell eggs. Roll each one in flour to coat. Set aside. Combine sausage, onions and parsley in a large bowl. Season with salt and pepper; mix well. Divide into 6 equal portions; flatten into thin rounds. Place 1 hard-cooked egg in the center of each round; cover completely with sausage, patting it well. Dip in beaten eggs, then coat with bread crumbs, patting crumbs on carefully. Refrigerate, covered with plastic wrap, up to 8 hours. To cook, heat 3 inches of oil in a deep-fryer. Fry eggs 1 or 2 at a time, turning, about 7 minutes, until crisp and brown, transferring to paper towels to drain. Serve hot or chilled, whole or halved, plain or with mustard.

Anchovy Squares

Scots are fond of anchovies as a flavoring and used in pastes for spreading on bread or toast. These squares can be served as appetizers or with afternoon tea.

Makes 24 squares

> 1 can (2 ounces) anchovy fillets, drained, rinsed
>
> 3 tablespoons butter, softened, cut in small pieces
>
> 2 teaspoons fresh lemon juice
>
> 1 teaspoon Dijon-style mustard
>
> Freshly ground pepper to taste
>
> 6 slices hot buttered toast, crusts removed

Purée anchovies, butter, lemon juice, mustard and pepper in an electric blender or food processor. Spoon mixture into a small dish. Refrigerate, covered with plastic wrap, several hours, up to 2 days. Leave at room temperature 30 minutes before serving. Spread each slice of toast with some of the anchovy mixture, dividing equally. Cut each slice into 4 squares.

Oat-Cheese Balls

These small rounds can be made with Scotland's distinctive creamy-white hard Dunlop cheese, originally made in an Ayrshire village of that name, or Cheddar cheese.

Makes 20

> ¼ cup rolled oats (quick or old-fashioned)
>
> ½ cup (1 stick) butter, softened
>
> 1 cup finely grated Dunlop or Cheddar cheese
>
> 1 teaspoon Worcestershire sauce
>
> ⅛ teaspoon paprika
>
> Salt, freshly ground pepper to taste

Toast oats in a dry small skillet over medium heat until lightly browned, stirring, about 3 minutes.

Combine butter, cheese, Worcestershire and paprika in a small bowl. Season with salt and pepper. Mix well. Chill 30 minutes. Shape into 20 small balls. Roll each cheese ball in toasted oats. Refrigerate until ready to serve.

Devils on Horseback

These broiled chutney-stuffed prunes, wrapped in bacon slices, are delectable appetizers or can be served for high tea.

Makes 16

> *16 pitted canned prunes*
> *About 2 tablespoons chutney*
> *8 bacon slices, halved crosswise*
> *About ⅓ cup grated Cheddar cheese*
> *16 small squares hot buttered toast*

Stuff each prune with a little chutney. Wrap a half slice of bacon around each prune. Put on a broiler rack. Sprinkle tops with grated cheese. Put under a hot broiler until crisp, then turn over to crisp on other side. Drain on paper toweling. Place a prune on each toast square. Serve at once.

Scotch Woodcock

There's nary a woodcock in these scrambled eggs served on anchovy toast. Once a favorite savory, it can be served as a first course for luncheon or as a breakfast dish.

Serves 4

> 8 egg yolks
> 1 cup heavy cream
> ⅛ teaspoon cayenne pepper
> Freshly ground pepper to taste
> 3 tablespoons butter
> 4 slices hot buttered toast
> 4 teaspoons anchovy paste
> 8 flat anchovy fillets, drained
> 2 teaspoons chopped fresh parsley

Whisk egg yolks, cream and cayenne in a small dish. Season with pepper.

Melt butter in a medium skillet; pour in egg mixture. Cook over low heat, stirring gently, until soft and creamy. Quickly spread each slice of toast with 1 teaspoon anchovy paste. Arrange on individual plates. Spoon an equal portion of scrambled eggs over toast. Crisscross 2 anchovy fillets over each portion. Sprinkle each with ½ teaspoon parsley. Serve at once.

Soups

The Scots have a wealth of imaginative soups that range from the hearty Scotch broth to an elegant chilled avocado potage. Soup-making has long been one of the special skills of the Scottish housewife, who utilized the bounty of land and sea to create a marvelous repertoire of national favorites.

The names of many Scottish soups are as imaginative as their ingredients. Powsowdie is sheep's head broth; skink, a vegetable-beef soup; feather fowlie, a creamy chicken soup; nettle kail, a cockerel, nettle and oat soup; and bawd bree, a hare soup.

H.V. Morton wrote a fine accolade to two special Scottish soups, stating that he could "live on Scotch broth and cocky-leekie for ever. These supreme soups, the absolute monarchs of the stock-pot, are unparalleled elsewhere in the world. They are the food of the Gods."

Cock-a-Leekie

Featuring chicken and leeks, this famous soup acquired its name probably because it was made with a cockerel or young rooster in the days when cock fighting was a popular sport and the defeated bird ended up in the soup pot. This is a modern recipe.

Serves 8

> 1 bunch (3 to 4 medium) leeks
> 2 chicken breast halves (about 1½ pounds), skinned
> 1 small onion, finely chopped
> 1 medium bay leaf
> ½ teaspoon dried thyme
> Salt, pepper to taste
> 2 cups rich chicken broth
> 1 cup light cream
> ½ cup chopped fresh parsley

Cut roots and top green leaves from leeks. Split white parts lengthwise; rinse thoroughly under running water to remove all dirt. Drain; slice thinly.

Put chicken breasts, onion, bay leaf and thyme in a large skillet. Season with salt and pepper. Add cold water to cover chicken by 1 inch. Bring to a boil; reduce heat; cook slowly about 10 minutes, until chicken is tender. Remove chicken from skillet; set aside to cool; strain and reserve broth. Remove and discard chicken skin and bones; cut meat into bite-size cubes.

Measure reserved broth; add enough water, if necessary, to make 3 cups liquid. Pour into a large saucepan; bring to a boil; add sliced leeks. Reduce heat; cook slowly about 10 minutes, until tender. Add chicken broth; heat to a boil; reduce heat. Add cream and cubes of chicken. Season. Leave over low heat about 5 minutes. Garnish with parsley.

Partan Bree

This rich cream of crab soup originated with fishermen in the western Scottish islands. *Partan* is Gaelic for crab and *bree* means broth.

Serves 4

> 2 cups chicken broth
> ¼ cup long-grain rice
> 1 tablespoon butter
> 1 cup flaked, cleaned fresh crabmeat
> 1 flat anchovy fillet, minced, or 1
> teaspoon anchovy paste
> 2 cups hot milk
> ½ cup heavy cream
> Freshly ground white pepper to taste
> 2 tablespoons chopped fresh watercress

Combine chicken broth, rice and butter in a large saucepan. Bring to a boil; reduce heat. Cook slowly, covered, about 20 minutes, until rice is tender. Add ½ cup crabmeat and anchovy or paste. Purée in a food mill or processor. Return to rinsed saucepan; reheat over low heat. Add hot milk, cream and remaining ½ cup crabmeat. Season with pepper. Cook slowly 1 or 2 minutes. Serve garnished with watercress.

Cullen Skink

This inviting soup is made with smoked haddock, popularly called finnan haddie. *Skink* is an old Gaelic word for broth and Cullen is a picturesque fishing village and resort town on the Moray Firth in northeastern Scotland. The soup is enriched with milk, butter and mashed potatoes.

Serves 8

> 1 medium onion, finely chopped
>
> 4 tablespoons butter
>
> 1 finnan haddie (smoked haddock), about 2 pounds
>
> 2 cups boiling water
>
> 1 cup mashed cooked potatoes
>
> 3 cups milk
>
> Salt, pepper to taste
>
> 1/2 cup heavy cream
>
> 2 tablespoons chopped watercress or chives

Sauté onion in 2 tablespoons melted butter in a large saucepan until tender. Add finnan haddie, cut in 3 or 4 pieces, and boiling water. Cook slowly, covered, about 20 minutes, until fish is tender. Remove fish and flake, discarding skin and bones. Strain liquid; return to rinsed saucepan; heat until hot. Add mashed potatoes, milk and 2 tablespoons butter. Season with salt and pepper. Blend until smooth. Add cream and flaked fish. Heat slowly 2 to 3 minutes. Serve garnished with watercress or chives.

Tomato-Orange Potage

This velvety orange-flavored fresh tomato soup is a specialty in Scottish country inns. It can be served hot or cold.

Serves 8

> 2 pounds (about 3 large) ripe red tomatoes
>
> 1 cup finely chopped onions
>
> 1 cup finely chopped carrots
>
> 4 cups rich chicken broth
>
> 1 teaspoon dried basil
>
> 1 medium bay leaf
>
> Salt, pepper to taste
>
> 3 tablespoons butter
>
> 2 tablespoons all-purpose flour
>
> ½ cup fresh orange juice
>
> 1 teaspoon grated orange rind
>
> ½ cup heavy cream

Peel, seed and chop tomatoes. Combine with onions, carrots, chicken broth, basil and bay leaf in a large saucepan. Season with salt and pepper. Bring to a boil; reduce heat. Cook slowly, covered, 30 minutes. Remove from heat. Remove and discard bay leaf. Purée mixture in a food mill or processor.

Melt butter in rinsed saucepan; stir in flour; cook, stirring, 1 minute. Stir in tomato purée; add orange juice and rind. Bring to a boil; reduce heat. Cook slowly, covered, 10 minutes. Add cream. Heat 1 minute. Serve hot, or cool and refrigerate to chill. Serve topped with dollops of whipped cream, if desired.

Tattie Brö

Every Scottish cook has a favorite recipe for a potato or "tattie" soup. Here's mine.

Serves 8 to 10

1 pound (about 4 medium) potatoes
1 pound (about 4 medium) white turnips
1 cup finely chopped onions
2 tablespoons butter
6 cups water
1 cup finely chopped carrots
1 teaspoon dried thyme
Salt, pepper to taste
1 cup sour cream
2 cups milk
¼ cup chopped fresh parsley

Peel and cut potatoes and turnips into small cubes.

Sauté onions in melted butter in a large saucepan until tender. Add water, potatoes, turnips, carrots and thyme. Season with salt and pepper. Bring to a boil; reduce heat. Cook slowly, covered, about 20 minutes, until vegetables are tender. Purée mixture in food mill or processor. Return purée to rinsed saucepan; reheat over low heat. Add sour cream and milk. Heat slowly about 5 minutes. Serve garnished with parsley.

Feather Fowlie

This is a modern version of a creamy chicken soup that was introduced to Scotland by French cooks. *Fowlie* derives from *volaille*, fowl.

Serves 6 to 8

5 cups water
1 small onion, minced
¼ cup diced cooked ham
1 medium stalk celery, with leaves, chopped
½ teaspoon dried thyme
2 chicken breast halves (about 1½ pounds), skinned
Salt, pepper to taste
1 cup frozen green peas
1 medium carrot, cut into thin slivers
2 egg yolks
½ cup heavy cream
⅛ teaspoon freshly grated nutmeg

Put water, onion, ham, celery and leaves, and thyme in a large skillet. Bring to a boil; reduce heat. Add chicken breasts. Season with salt and pepper. Cook slowly, covered, about 10 minutes, until chicken is tender. Remove chicken from skillet; set aside to cool. Strain broth into a large saucepan. Remove and discard chicken skin and bones; cut chicken into small julienne pieces.

Heat chicken broth; add chicken pieces, peas and carrot slivers. Heat 2 to 3 minutes. Meanwhile, whisk egg yolks with cream in a small dish; add nutmeg and a large spoonful of hot soup, whisking as adding. Add to soup, whisking as adding. Leave over low heat 2 to 3 minutes. Serve at once.

Lorraine Soup

This almond-flavored soup can be traced back to the days of friendship between France and Scotland. It is said to be named after Mary of Lorraine, mother of Mary Queen of Scots. Mine is an adaptation of an old Scottish recipe.

Serves 6 to 8

1½ cups chopped cooked chicken
½ cup blanched almonds
2 hard-cooked egg yolks
4 cups chicken broth
3 tablespoons white bread crumbs
½ teaspoon grated lemon rind
⅛ teaspoon grated nutmeg
Salt, freshly ground white pepper to taste
2 cups light cream
2 tablespoons chopped chives

Purée chicken, almonds and egg yolks in a food mill or processor. Turn into a large saucepan; add chicken broth and bread crumbs; mix well. Bring to a boil; reduce heat. Add lemon rind and nutmeg. Season with salt and pepper. Simmer, covered, 10 minutes. Add cream. Heat until hot. Do not boil. Serve garnished with chives.

Oatmeal-Buttermilk Brose

Scots make simple, creamy, nutty-flavored oatmeal soups that are surprisingly good. This is one of them.

Serves 4 to 6

¼ cup rolled oats

1 cup finely chopped onions

1 cup finely chopped carrots

3 tablespoons butter

2 cups chicken broth

Salt, pepper to taste

2 cups buttermilk

2 tablespoons chopped fresh parsley

Toast oats in a dry small skillet, stirring over medium heat until lightly browned, about 3 minutes.

Sauté onions and carrots in melted butter in a large saucepan 5 minutes. Stir in oats. Cook, stirring frequently, 4 minutes. Gradually add chicken broth, stirring as adding. Season with salt and pepper. Cook slowly, covered, 25 minutes. Purée mixture in a food mill or processor. Return to rinsed saucepan. Add buttermilk. Heat until hot. Do not boil. Serve garnished with parsley.

Seafood

Among Scotland's gastronomic pleasures, none is more delightful than the seafood. Scots have a varied and bountiful harvest of fish and shellfish to use in their innovative dishes. Off the Scottish coasts is some of the best sea-fishing in the world. Rivers, streams and lochs teem with exceptional fish, including the matchless salmon and trout.

Fish has long been an all-important Scottish food, eaten fresh or cured in what became the traditional way: with a touch of the elements. Using techniques for salting and smoking introduced by the Norsemen, Scots developed exceptional products that became world renowned. There are many kinds, ranging from the everyday smokie to the luxurious smoked salmon.

Scots still enjoy their down-to-earth traditional dishes such as Crappit Heids (oatmeal-stuffed haddock heads) and Ham and Haddie (smoked haddock topped with fried ham slices) as well as elegant creations like lobster with Drambuie and turbot adorned with watercress sauce. Two unusual favorites are Haggamuggie (a Shetland fish haggis) and Graved Lax (fresh salmon marinated with dill, peppercorns, rock salt and sugar in the manner of the Vikings). In Scotland there are also superb oyster, clam and mussel soup-stews, pies and creamed dishes.

Scots enjoy seafood for all meals, especially their great substantial breakfast or morning banquet, which always includes a selection of hot and cold specialties.

Salmon

The succulent salmon, long prized in Scotland and once so abundant that it was an inexpensive everyday food, is the king of fish both for eating and sport. It is taken from the Atlantic and the famous Scottish rivers—the Dee, Spey, Tay and Tweed.

Salmon has a rich flavor and is fine in texture, yet firm and moist. Properly cooked, it is a gastronomic treat. The simplest methods of cooking are best: boiling, steaming, baking and grilling (for steaks). There is no equal to poached fresh salmon, cooked gently in salted water and served with lemon juice and butter or a flavorful shrimp, anchovy or lobster sauce.

Sir Walter Scott did not agree, however. He wrote, "The most judicious gastronomes eat no other sauce than a spoonful of the water in which the salmon has been boiled, together with a little pepper and vinegar."

Early Scots enjoyed pickled, potted and spiced salmon as well as salmon fritters and cakes.

Tweed Kettle

This flavorful salmon "hash" is a 19th-century specialty that was made originally in country inns near the Tweed River in the Borders region.

Serves 4

> 2 pounds fresh salmon
>
> 1 cup dry white wine
>
> 2 tablespoons minced chives
>
> 1/8 teaspoon freshly grated nutmeg
>
> Salt, pepper to taste
>
> 2 tablespoons butter
>
> 2 cups chopped fresh mushrooms
>
> 2 tablespoons chopped fresh dill

Cut salmon into 2-inch cubes. Put in a large saucepan. Add wine, chives and nutmeg. Season with salt and pepper. Cook slowly, covered, about 5 minutes, until just tender.

Meanwhile, melt butter in a small skillet. Add mushrooms and sauté 2 minutes. Add to salmon mixture. Stir in dill. Cook slowly 1 minute. Serve with creamed potatoes.

Kedgeree

This is the Scottish version of the popular English breakfast dish that originated in India. It is usually made with salmon or finnan haddie.

Serves 4 to 6

> 3 tablespoons butter
> 1 teaspoon curry powder
> 1 tablespoon fresh lemon juice
> 2 cups cooked flaked salmon
> 2 cups cooked white rice
> 2 hard-cooked eggs, finely chopped
> ½ cup light cream
> ⅛ teaspoon cayenne pepper
> Salt, freshly ground pepper to taste
> ⅓ cup chopped fresh parsley

Melt butter in a large saucepan; stir in curry powder and lemon juice; cook 1 minute. Add salmon; sauté 2 or 3 minutes. Stir in rice, eggs, cream and cayenne. Season with salt and pepper. Cook over medium heat, tossing lightly with a fork, until hot. Stir in parsley. Serve shaped into a mound on a platter.

Herring

The nutritious, small saltwater fish called herring has been a staple food in Scotland for centuries. "It's nae fish ye're buying, it's men's lives," wrote Sir Walter Scott.

Scots enjoy herring fresh, smoked or salted in a variety of good dishes.

Fresh, the herring can be potted, pickled, grilled and served with mustard sauce, or fried after rolling in oatmeal. Two interesting specialties are Glasgow Magistrates (plump stuffed and baked herrings that are said to resemble courtroom officials) and Tatties an' Herrin (boiled new-jacket potatoes topped with herrings and steamed).

Kippers

One of Scotland's most famous and beloved foods is kippers, or kippered herring. They have an exclusive taste and Scots around the world yearn to eat them.

When split open and flattened, the fish are then salted and smoked, acquiring a copper color and desirable strong smoky flavor. The finest come from Scotland's west coast. The large and fleshy, mildly smoked Loch Fyne kippers are the most highly prized. Also excellent are small and plump Mallaig kippers that have a rich chestnut brown color.

Ask a Scot about kippers and he will describe them with an affectionate eloquence. For they are revered as a delicacy rather than a commonplace food.

Kippers are eaten fried in butter, baked or poached in milk, or broiled, either plain or sometimes with a butter-lemon sauce. They are a special breakfast dish, often served with scrambled eggs and oatcakes.

Broiled Kippers

Kippers purchased in the United States come from Canada as well as Scotland and should be prepared according to the package instructions. Allow 1 or 2 kippers per person. Generally they are placed on a broiler rack, spread with softened butter and sprinkled with pepper and then broiled, according to their plumpness, from 3 to 7 minutes, or until the skin curls up and is crisp and brown. Serve with a wedge of lemon.

For Kipper Toast, a favorite breakfast or high tea dish, place kippers on buttered toast and top with a poached egg.

Finnan Haddie

The popular name for smoked salted haddock is finnan haddie, which comes from the village of Findon (pronounced finnan) in Kincairdireshe where the fisherfolk originated the now-famous method of smoking the fish over a peat fire.

Finnan haddie has a pale golden color and soft tender flesh with a mild but assertive smoky flavor. Because it is lightly salted the fish does not require soaking before cooking. Scots like it broiled (spread with butter) and served hot and crisp with pats of butter and pepper. They are also devotees of the fish poached in milk and served with mustard sauce.

Scots use cooked and flaked finnans to make creative soufflés and casseroles, to add to scrambled eggs or omelets, to mix with mashed potatoes for fish cakes, and to make creamed dishes, salads and pâtés. Fried finnans and ham and Egganhaddie (poached fish topped with a poached egg and served with grilled tomatoes) are breakfast favorites.

Aberdeen Nips

This creamed dish is from the major fishing port of Aberdeen, situated on the North Sea between the Dee and Don rivers.

Serves 4

> 2 tablespoons butter
>
> 2 tablespoons all-purpose flour
>
> 2 cups light cream or milk
>
> 2 cups flaked cooked smoked haddock (finnan haddie)
>
> Pinch of cayenne and black peppers
>
> 3 large egg yolks, beaten
>
> 4 slices hot buttered toast
>
> Chopped fresh parsley

Melt butter in a medium saucepan over low heat. Stir in flour; cook 1 minute. Gradually add cream or milk, stirring constantly. Cook until thickened and smooth. Add haddock and the peppers; stir in egg yolks; cook 1 minute.

Spoon an equal portion of fish mixture over each toast slice. Sprinkle with parsley. Serve at once.

Arbroath Smokies

Smokies are fresh haddocks that have been cleaned, cured and smoked whole (not flattened like kippers). They originated in the picturesque fishing village of Auchmithie, perched on a cliff overlooking the North Sea. Later the villagers relocated a few miles south in Arbroath and that name became associated with the smokies.

The hot-smoking process gives the fish a deep copper color, a strong smoky flavor and a soft textured flesh. Smokies are usually bought in pairs, tied together at the tails.

Because smokies are already cooked, they can be eaten cold but taste better reheated briefly in a 450° oven or under a broiler. The skinned, boned and flaked fish is excellent for making omelets and creamed dishes and a Smokie Cocotte (topped with cream, chopped tomatoes and grated cheese and baked).

Smokies are favorite snacks and breakfast specialties and are served with baked or boiled potatoes for high tea.

Trout Fried in Oatmeal

Delicate river trout, coated with oatmeal and pan fried, has been a favorite breakfast dish in Scotland's Borders region for years.

Wash and dry a cleaned trout, allowing one per person. Dip each one in milk and then roll in oatmeal (rolled oats) seasoned with salt and pepper.

Melt 2 tablespoons of butter per fish in a heavy skillet. Add trout and fry on both sides until flesh flakes easily with a fork and is well browned. Serve at once with a pat of butter and lemon wedge and oatcakes, if desired.

Cabbie Claw

This poached cod dish is from the Shetland Islands. There a codling is called *kabbilow*, from the French *cabillaud*, meaning fresh cod.

Serves 4

> 1 pound fresh cod fillets
> 1 cup boiling water
> 1 tablespoon white vinegar
> 2 teaspoons grated fresh or prepared horseradish, drained
> 3 tablespoons chopped fresh parsley
> Salt, pepper to taste
> 2 tablespoons butter
> 2 tablespoons all-purpose flour
> 1 cup milk
> 1 tablespoon Dijon-style mustard
> 2 hard-cooked eggs, finely chopped
> 2 cups warm seasoned mashed potatoes

Place cod fillets in a large skillet. Pour in boiling water. Add vinegar, horseradish and 1 tablespoon parsley. Season with salt and pepper. Simmer gently, covered, about 7 minutes, until fish is tender. Transfer to a serving dish; keep warm. Strain liquid and reserve.

Melt butter in a medium saucepan. Stir in flour; cook 1 minute. Gradually add fish liquid and milk, stirring as adding. Stir in mustard. Season with salt and pepper. Cook slowly, stirring, until thickened and smooth. Add eggs. Cook 1 minute. Pour over cod fillets. Sprinkle with remaining 2 tablespoons parsley. Form a border around dish with mashed potatoes.

Hebridean Fisherman's Pie

Fish pies are a popular Scottish dish and can be made with any kind of cooked fish. The covering can be pastry or mashed potatoes. This attractive specialty is an adaptation of a dish from the Hebridean island of Skye, noted for its dramatic landscape and legends.

Serves 4

> 1 pound haddock or sole fillets
> 1 cup milk
> Salt, pepper to taste
> 3 tablespoons butter
> 4 green onions, with some tops, chopped
> 1/4 pound fresh mushrooms, cleaned and sliced
> 2 tablespoons fresh lemon juice
> Pinch cayenne pepper
> 3 tablespoons all-purpose flour
> 1/2 cup dry white wine
> 1/8 teaspoon grated nutmeg
> 1 large tomato, peeled, halved, sliced
> 2 hard-cooked eggs, sliced
> 2 cups warm seasoned mashed potatoes
> 2 tablespoons melted butter

Place fish fillets in a large skillet. Pour in milk. Season with salt and pepper. Bring to a gentle simmer. Simmer, covered, about 7 minutes, until fish is just tender. Transfer fish to a buttered deep baking dish. Reserve liquid.

Melt butter in a medium saucepan. Add onions; sauté until tender. Add mushrooms, lemon juice and cayenne; sauté 2 minutes. Stir in flour. Continue cooking 1 minute. Gradually add reserved liquid, stirring as adding. Add wine and nutmeg. Season with salt and pepper. Cook slowly until thickened and smooth. Pour over fish fillets. Arrange tomato slices over the fish. Top with egg slices. Form a border around dish with mashed potatoes. Brush with melted butter. Bake in a preheated 350° oven for about 25 minutes, until bubbly hot and golden brown.

Partan Pie

This is a Scottish version of deviled crab.

Serves 4

> *3 cups crabmeat, preferably lump, picked over*
>
> *⅛ teaspoon freshly grated nutmeg*
>
> *Salt, pepper to taste*
>
> *3 tablespoons fresh lemon juice*
>
> *1 tablespoon prepared Dijon-style mustard*
>
> *⅓ cup freshly made bread crumbs*
>
> *⅓ cup melted butter*

Combine crabmeat and nutmeg in a medium bowl. Season with salt and pepper. Stir in remaining ingredients. Spoon into 4 crab shells or individual ramekins. Bake in a preheated 375° oven for 20 minutes, until bubbly hot and golden brown.

Scallops in Coffins

The "coffins" in this recipe are baked potatoes.

Serves 4

4 hot large baked potatoes
¼ cup (½ stick) butter
2 teaspoons fresh lemon juice
1 teaspoon curry powder
2 tablespoons all-purpose flour
1 cup light cream
Salt, pepper to taste
2 tablespoons minced green pepper
2 cups diced, cooked sea scallops
2 teaspoons chopped fresh parsley

Cut a lengthwise slice from the top of each potato. Scoop out potato contents; use for another dish.

Melt butter in a medium saucepan. Add lemon juice and curry powder; sauté 1 minute. Stir in flour; cook 1 minute. Gradually add cream, stirring as adding. Season with salt and pepper. Cook slowly until thickened and smooth. Stir in green pepper and scallops. Cook 1 or 2 minutes to heat. Carefully spoon scallop mixture into potato shells. Garnish tops with parsley. Place in a shallow baking dish. Bake in a preheated 400° oven about 15 minutes, until hot and tops are golden.

Hairy Tatties

This is another old-time dish with a curious name—harried potatoes. In Gaelic *hairy* means to harry. The ingredients are leftover mashed potatoes and cod fish.

Serves 6

> ½ *cup rolled oats*
> 2 *cups shredded cooked codfish*
> 2 *cups warm mashed potatoes*
> 2 *tablespoons butter, melted*
> 2 *teaspoons Dijon-style mustard*
> 2 *teaspoons Worcestershire sauce*
> *Pepper to taste*
> 1 *large tomato, sliced*

Toast oats in a small dry skillet over medium heat until lightly browned, stirring, about 3 minutes. Set aside.

Combine codfish, potatoes, butter, mustard and Worcestershire in a medium bowl. Season with pepper. Mix well.

Spoon into a large shallow baking dish, spreading evenly. Top with tomato slices. Sprinkle with toasted oats. Bake in a preheated 400° oven about 15 minutes, until hot and bubbly.

Meat, Poultry and Game

Scotland is famous for its superior Galloway and Aberdeen Angus cattle. The celebrated "Roast Beef of Old England" has, for generations, been Scottish in origin. Scots have their own names for cuts of meat that take a bit of inside knowledge to figure out: fleshy end, heughbone steak, softside and pope's eye.

Scots are very fond of their sweet-tasting lamb. Roast and broiled lamb are served with gravy, red currant or rowan jelly; fresh mint sauce is the favorite accompaniment for spring lamb.

The Scottish tradition of making small amounts of food go a long way and for utilizing leftovers has resulted in superb Scotch pies, puddings, loaves and pasties, especially Forfar bridies, said to have been created by an Angus baker called Mr. Jolly. Once sold at farmers' markets, they are now popular fare at Scottish Games or Gatherings. Those with one hole in the bridie have only meat inside; those with two holes include onions.

Although some of the poultry dishes have a notable French influence, the names are definitely Scottish. One called Friar's Chicken, created by cooks of the holy orders, is made with a cinnamon-flavored veal and chicken broth, enriched with egg yolks. H.V. Morton acclaimed it as a "great and romantic food," and "a dish to banish melancholy." Roastit Bubbly-Jock (the name for a turkey

47

cock) is a turkey stuffed with sausage and chestnuts.

Throughout Scotland superb wild game, such as the great red deer, and noble birds, especially the grouse, pheasant and partridge, are found in the vast forests and moors. Cooks have long had a special talent for preparing them in mouthwatering dishes flavored with herbs, spirits and condiments.

Collops-in-the-Pan

Collops, or escalopes, are thin slices of veal or beef that Scots cook in a spicy sauce. This specialty includes oats.

Serves 4

3 tablespoons rolled oats

1 pound top round steak, thinly sliced

Salt, pepper to taste

2 tablespoons butter

1 medium onion, thinly sliced

1 cup beef broth

1 tablespoon Worcestershire sauce

⅛ teaspoon freshly grated nutmeg

2 tablespoons chopped fresh parsley

Toast oats in a small dry skillet over medium heat until lightly browned, stirring, about 3 minutes. Cool.

Cut off any fat from the steak. Slice into escalopes about 3 inches square. Sprinkle with salt and pepper.

Melt butter in a large skillet. Add steak squares; brown on both sides. Remove to a plate. Add onion slices to drippings; sauté until tender. Return steak to skillet. Add broth, Worcestershire and nutmeg. Stir in oats. Cook slowly, covered, 10 minutes. Serve garnished with parsley.

Whisky Steaks

These Gaelic steaks are flavored with pepper and Scotch whisky.

Serves 4

2 tablespoons butter

2 tablespoons vegetable oil

1 large onion, cut crosswise and sliced thinly

4 center-cut fillet steaks

½ cup beef broth

½ teaspoon freshly ground pepper

¼ cup Scotch whisky

Heat butter and oil in a large skillet. Add onion slices; sauté until tender. Remove to a plate and keep warm. Add steaks to drippings and sear over high heat 1 minute on each side. Reduce heat to low and cook steaks about 4 minutes on each side for medium-rare. Remove to warm plates.

Increase heat to high. Add beef broth, stirring and scraping up all browned bits on the bottom. Cook 2 to 3 minutes, until broth is reduced by half. Season with pepper. Add whisky. Heat 1 minute. Pour over steaks. Garnish with onions. Serve with a pat of butter on top of each one, if desired.

Mince and Tatties

Mince is the Scottish hamburger. It is served with mashed potatoes or tatties as a popular supper dish.

Serves 4

1 tablespoon beef drippings or butter
1 medium onion, finely chopped
1 pound lean ground beef
½ cup beef broth
1 tablespoon rolled oats
1 tablespoon Worcestershire sauce
Pepper to taste

Heat beef drippings or butter in a large skillet. Add onion; sauté until tender. Add beef and brown quickly, stirring, until redness disappears. Add broth, oats and Worcestershire. Season with pepper. Cook slowly, covered, 15 minutes.

Tuppeny Struggles

This farmhouse dish, made with cubed left-over roast lamb in a flavorful gravy and topped with a mashed potato crust, is the Scottish version of Shepherd's Pie.

Serves 4

> 4 tablespoons butter
>
> 2 teaspoons curry powder
>
> 1 medium onion, finely chopped
>
> 2 cups brown gravy
>
> 1 tablespoon Worcestershire sauce
>
> ½ teaspoon dried marjoram
>
> Pepper to taste
>
> 3 cups cubed cooked lamb
>
> 2 cups seasoned mashed potatoes
>
> Paprika

Melt 2 tablespoons butter in a medium saucepan. Add curry powder and onion; sauté until tender. Add gravy, Worcestershire and marjoram. Season with pepper. Cook slowly 5 minutes to blend flavors. Stir in lamb; cook another 5 minutes. Spoon into a 2½-quart casserole. Top with potatoes, spreading evenly. Dot top with bits of remaining 2 tablespoons of butter. Sprinkle lightly with paprika. Bake in a preheated 400° oven about 25 minutes, until bubbly hot and top is golden brown.

Hotch Potch

A lamb-vegetable stew, also called harvest pot, this one-dish meal is famous in song and story. The lines of a ditty called "A Song in Praise of Hodge Podge" mentions a long list of ingredients: carrots, turnips, onions, leeks, barley, peas, beets and beans as well as "hearty wholesome meats." This is a modified version.

Serves 4

> 3 pounds neck or breast of lamb, cut up
>
> 2 tablespoons vegetable oil
>
> Salt, pepper to taste
>
> About 1 cup beef broth or water
>
> 2 large carrots, scraped and sliced
>
> 2 large onions, quartered
>
> 2 cups shelled green peas
>
> 6 green onions, with some tops, sliced
>
> 1 teaspoon sugar
>
> 1 tablespoon chopped fresh mint

Brown lamb pieces in heated oil in a large kettle. Season with salt and pepper. Add beef broth or water. Simmer, covered, 1 hour, adding more liquid if needed. Add carrots and onions. Continue cooking 30 minutes longer. Add remaining ingredients and cook about 15 minutes, or until lamb and vegetables are tender.

Inky Pinky

This recipe is an adaptation of one in *The Cook and Housewife's Manual,* a cookbook and household guide that was published in Edinburgh in 1826. It is one of several using leftover cooked meat.

Serves 4 to 6

    2 tablespoons butter

    1 medium onion, finely chopped

    1½ cups beef gravy

    1 tablespoon vinegar

    Salt, pepper to taste

    3 cups cubed cooked beef

    1 cup diced cooked carrots

    2 tablespoons chopped fresh parsley

Melt butter in a medium saucepan. Add onion; sauté until tender. Add gravy and vinegar. Season with salt and pepper. Heat to boiling. Lower heat; add beef and carrots. Cook slowly, covered, 10 minutes. Stir in parsley. Serve over hot buttered toast slices or with mashed potatoes.

Poor Man's Pie

This is a baked sausage-oat-vegetable dish that hails from a friend in the Highlands.

Serves 6

> 1 pound pork sausage meat
> ½ cup minced onions
> ½ cup minced carrots
> ½ cup minced celery
> 1 cup rolled oats
> ½ cup applesauce
> 1 egg, beaten
> 2 teaspoons Dijon-style prepared mustard
> 1 teaspoon Worcestershire sauce
> ½ teaspoon ground allspice
> Dash of pepper

Combine ingredients thoroughly in a large bowl. Spoon into a shallow baking dish. Bake in a preheated 375° oven 1 hour, or until ingredients are cooked. Serve with mashed potatoes.

Happit Hen

The original recipe for this dish was made with chicken poached in broth with vegetables. *Happit* is the Gaelic word for covered. This is a modern version.

Serves 4

> ¼ cup butter
> 1 medium onion, finely chopped
> 2 medium carrots, scraped and chopped
> 1 cup diced celery
> 3 tablespoons all-purpose flour
> 2 cups chicken broth
> ½ teaspoon dried marjoram
> Salt, pepper to taste
> ½ cup light cream
> 2 cups diced cooked chicken

Melt butter in a medium saucepan; add onion, carrots and celery. Cook slowly about 5 minutes, until vegetables are soft. Stir in flour; cook 1 minute. Gradually add chicken broth, stirring as adding. Add marjoram. Season with salt and pepper. Cook slowly, covered, about 10 minutes, until thickened and smooth. Add cream and chicken. Cook another 2 minutes. Serve over hot cooked rice.

Stoved Howtowdie

This French-inspired 19th-century stuffed pot-roasted chicken was originally an elaborate creation called Howtowdie wi' Drappit Eggs. *Howtowdie* meant a young chicken that had never laid an egg. *Drappit* was the word for poached.

Serves 4 to 6

> 1 roasting chicken, about 5 pounds
> Oatmeal Stuffing (recipe across)
> 1/2 lemon
> 1/4 cup butter
> 1/2 cup finely chopped onions
> 3 cups chicken broth
> 3 whole allspice
> 1 medium bay leaf
> Salt, pepper to taste
> 2 tablespoons light cream

Wash and dry chicken; stuff body and neck cavities lightly with oatmeal stuffing; truss. Rub skin all over with cut side of lemon.

Melt butter in a casserole or pot large enough to hold the chicken. Add chicken and brown lightly on all sides, turning carefully with two spoons so skin is not torn. Add onions, chicken broth, allspice and bay leaf. Season with salt and pepper. Cook, covered, in a preheated 375° oven about 1 hour, or until chicken is tender. Transfer to a warm platter; keep warm. Strain broth and drippings into a small saucepan; heat. Add cream; heat slowly 1 minute. Pour over chicken. Serve surrounded with small mounds of creamed spinach, if desired.

Oatmeal Stuffing

3 tablespoons butter
1 cup finely chopped onions
1½ cups rolled oats
½ teaspoon dried thyme
3 tablespoons chopped fresh parsley
Salt, pepper to taste
2 tablespoons milk

Melt butter in a medium saucepan; add onions; sauté until tender. Stir in oats, thyme and parsley. Season with salt and pepper. Cook over medium heat, stirring, about 3 minutes, until oats are lightly browned. Stir in milk. Remove from heat.

Wet Devil

Devilling, or cooking with mustard, was a popular old technique of treating meats and poultry. This recipe for breast of chicken in a flavorful "wet" sauce dates back to the 1880s.

Serves 6

1/2 cup (1 stick) butter, softened

1 tablespoon Worcestershire sauce

1 tablespoon fresh lemon juice

2 tablespoons Dijon-style prepared mustard

1 teaspoon dry mustard

2 teaspoons curry powder

Pinch cayenne pepper

Freshly ground black pepper

3 whole chicken breasts, cut in halves, skinned

2 tablespoons vegetable oil

1 large onion, finely chopped

1 1/4 cups chicken broth

1/4 cup heavy cream

1/4 cup chopped fresh parsley

Cream butter in a medium dish. Add Worcestershire, lemon juice, mustards, curry powder and peppers. Beat until thoroughly combined.

Pat chicken dry with paper towels. Spread both sides with butter-mustard mixture. Leave at room temperature 30 minutes.

Heat oil in a large skillet. Add onion; sauté until tender. Add chicken breasts and brown lightly on both sides. Pour in chicken broth. Cook slowly, covered, about 25 minutes, or until tender. Add cream during the last minute of cooking. Stir in parsley. Serve chicken breasts with the sauce spooned over them.

Roast Grouse

Although Scots relish all species of grouse—
the capercailzie (or wood), the ptarmigan (or
white) and the black—gastronomes regard
the red grouse as the finest game bird in the
world. Called simply grouse or Scotch grouse,
its natural habitat is wherever heather grows
on the moors in Scotland and northern England. The first grouse that falls each year on
the "Glorious Twelfth" of August heralds the
opening of the British shooting season and
is an important social event.

Red grouse has a rich, gamy individual flavor achieved from a diet of berries and
tender heather shoots. Young birds are best
roasted. They can be stuffed with raspberries, cranberries or rowanberries and topped
with sprigs of heather previously soaked in
whisky. Traditional accompaniments are
game chips (homemade potato chips), Bread
Sauce (recipe next page) and a watercress
garnish.

Serves 2

>   2 young grouse, about 1½ pounds each
>   Salt, pepper to taste
>   4 tablespoons butter
>   3 tablespoons lemon juice
>   1 cup berries
>   4 slices bacon

Sprinkle grouse inside and out with salt and
pepper. Combine butter and lemon juice. Put
half of the mixture and ½ cup berries inside
each cavity. Place breast side up in a roasting
pan. Cover each with 2 bacon slices; fasten
with wooden picks. Roast in a preheated 350°
oven about 40 minutes, until just tender. Remove from oven, take off bacon. Place each
bird over 2 rounds of crisply fried bread and
serve with any of the traditional accompaniments.

59

Bread Sauce
Makes about 1½ cups

1½ cups milk
1 small onion, stuck with 2 whole cloves
⅛ teaspoon freshly grated nutmeg
Salt, freshly ground white pepper to taste
1 cup fresh white bread crumbs
1 tablespoon butter
1 to 2 tablespoons heavy cream

Put milk, onion, nutmeg, salt and pepper in a small saucepan. Bring slowly to a boil. Remove from heat; leave to let onion steep for 30 minutes, then discard it. Return pan to stove; bring milk to a simmering point; stir in bread crumbs; simmer 3 minutes, whisking bread occasionally, until sauce thickens and is somewhat smooth. Stir in butter and cream. Serve at once.

Tipsy Pheasant

The pheasant, a highly prized, beautiful game bird, was introduced to Scotland by the Romans. Scots prefer to cook the young ones simply, roasted with a few flavorings. They also enjoy rich game pies made with pheasant.

Serves 6

> 2 young pheasants, 3 to 4 pounds each
> Salt, pepper to taste
> 1 medium onion, halved
> 2 sprigs of thyme
> ¼ cup butter, melted
> 1 cup dry white wine

Wipe pheasants with a damp cloth. Sprinkle inside and out with salt and pepper. Put an onion half and thyme sprig in cavity of each bird. Truss birds. Place breast side up on a rack in a roasting pan. Brush with melted butter. Pour in wine. Roast in a preheated 350° oven, allowing 25 minutes per pound, until tender, basting frequently. Transfer to a warm serving platter. Serve with a tart jelly, red cabbage or Bread Sauce (see recipe, page 60) and garnish with watercress.

Rob Roy's Pleasure

This is my version of a recipe from *The Scots Kitchen*. Rob Roy was a famous Highland cateran (robber), and perhaps he enjoyed a similar dish made of venison braised with vegetables and wine.

Serves 6 to 8

> 3 tablespoons bacon fat or butter
>
> 1 venison roast (leg or shoulder), about 4 pounds
>
> 2 medium onions, sliced
>
> 2 medium carrots, sliced
>
> 3 whole cloves
>
> 1 medium bay leaf
>
> ½ teaspoon dried thyme
>
> 2 parsley sprigs
>
> Salt, pepper to taste
>
> ½ cup beef broth
>
> 1½ cups dry white wine
>
> ½ cup red port
>
> Pinch cayenne pepper

Heat fat or butter in a large kettle. Brown roast on all sides, turning carefully with two spoons. Add onions, carrots, cloves, bay leaf, thyme and parsley. Season with salt and pepper. Pour in beef broth and white wine. Cook slowly, covered, 2½ to 3 hours, until meat is tender, depending on the cut and age of venison. Remove to a warm platter. Skim off excess fat. Remove and discard cloves and bay leaf. Add port and cayenne. Bring to a boil; scrape drippings; boil 2 minutes. Serve with sliced venison.

Vegetables and Salads

Scots have long paid homage to their basic vegetables by preparing them in nourishing dishes that are different. They also give them places of honor on the home table.

Because of its harsh northern climate, Scotland has had a limited variety of plants, roots and herbs from which to choose. Yet all of them, especially greens and leafy vegetables, have long been appreciated for their minerals and vitamins. Even nettles and seaweed are treasured foods in the Scottish Highlands and Islands.

Scotland is famous for its potatoes, which have a special flavor and colors of red, blue, purple and black as well as white and yellow. The humble vegetable has been a prized ingredient in a variety of dishes including soups, pancakes, breads and casseroles. Many potato dishes are flavored with herbs, milk, butter, cheese and oats.

Scots are partial to one of the oldest vegetable families, the onion. They relish specialties featuring or flavored with chives, leeks, scallions and onion varieties—white, yellow and red.

Highland Colcannon

This dish is an appealing combination of potatoes, carrots and cabbage and is a traditional Halloween specialty. Cooks hide a coin in it as a symbol of good luck.

Serves 6 to 8

> 1 pound (about 4 medium) potatoes
> 3 large carrots, scraped and quartered
> Salt
> 4 tablespoons butter
> 1 pound (about ½ head) cabbage, shredded
> ¾ cup hot milk
> Pepper to taste
> 10 green onions, with some tops, sliced
> ⅓ cup chopped fresh parsley

Peel and halve potatoes. Put potatoes and carrots in a large saucepan. Cover with boiling salted water. Cook slowly, covered, about 25 minutes, until tender. Transfer vegetables from liquid to a large bowl; mash; add 2 tablespoons butter; mash again.

Put cabbage into vegetable liquid. Cook slowly, covered, until tender but crisp, about 7 minutes. Transfer cabbage to mix with vegetables in bowl. Add hot milk and 2 tablespoons butter. Season with salt and pepper. Mix well. Add green onions and parsley; mix well. Serve each portion with a pat of butter in the center, if desired.

Orkney Clapshot

This traditional potato-turnip dish is from the Orkney Islands, off Scotland's northwest coast, an area originally settled by the Vikings. Serve with haggis or roast beef.

Serves 4 to 6

1 pound (about 4 medium) potatoes
¾ pound (about 3 medium) white turnips
Salt
3 tablespoons light cream
2 tablespoons butter
Pepper to taste
2 tablespoons chopped chives

Peel and cut potatoes and turnips into small cubes. Put in a large saucepan. Cover with boiling salted water. Cook slowly, covered, about 20 minutes, until tender. Drain. Turn into a large bowl; mash; add cream and butter. Season with salt and pepper; mash again. Serve at once sprinkled with chives.

Stovies

The word *stovies* comes from the French *étouf-fer*—to cook slowly in an enclosed pot. Also called stoved potatoes, some cooks prepare the dish with sliced potatoes; others leave them whole and add leftover cooked meat and a little gravy to them.

Serves 6

> *1 large onion*
> *2 tablespoons bacon drippings or butter*
> *2 pounds (about 12) small new potatoes, peeled*
> *½ cup meat broth or water*
> *Salt, pepper to taste*
> *½ cup toasted oats*

Cut onion into quarters; slice thinly. Sauté in heated drippings or melted butter in a large saucepan until tender.

Add potatoes and broth or water. Season with salt and pepper. Cook slowly, covered, about 25 minutes, until just tender. Sprinkle with toasted oats. Cook another 5 minutes. Serve at once.

Oaten Potato Cakes

Scots are fond of a variety of fried cakes made with potatoes. This is one of the best.

Makes 12 cakes

> 2 cups warm stiff mashed potatoes
> About 1 cup rolled oats
> Salt, pepper to taste
> About 1/3 cup melted butter

Mix potatoes and ½ cup rolled oats in a medium bowl. Season with salt and pepper. Add 1 to 2 tablespoons melted butter, adding more oats if needed, to make a firm but soft dough. Sprinkle a clean surface with oats. Turn out potato mixture on them. Roll out to a half-inch thickness. With a floured 2½-inch cutter, cut into 12 rounds. Sprinkle tops with rolled oats. Cook on both sides on a buttered hot griddle or in a skillet until golden brown. Serve hot with butter.

Pan Haggerty

These cheese-flavored potatoes are cooked in a pan in a ragged or topsy-turvy manner.

Serves 4 to 6

> *1 pound (about 4 medium) potatoes, peeled*
> *1 large onion*
> *2 tablespoons bacon drippings or fat*
> *1 cup grated sharp Cheddar cheese*
> *Salt, pepper to taste*
> *2 tablespoons butter*

Cut potatoes into paper-thin slices; pat dry. Cut onion into quarters; slice thinly. Heat drippings or fat in a heavy skillet. Arrange alternate layers of potato and onion slices and cheese, topping with cheese, in skillet. Sprinkle each layer with salt and pepper and dot with butter. Cook, covered, over moderate heat about 30 minutes, until potatoes are tender. Remove cover and brown under a hot broiler until golden on top. Serve in skillet.

Rumbledethumps

This dish is from Scotland's Borders region and is served as an entrée or accompaniment. Once rumbled meant "mixed" and thumped "bashed together." Hence the unusual name.

Serves 4 to 6

> 1 pound (about 4 medium) potatoes
> Salt
> 1/2 cup milk
> 3 tablespoons butter
> Pepper to taste
> 1 pound (about 1/2 head) cabbage, shredded
> 1 medium onion, finely chopped
> 3 tablespoons chopped chives or parsley
> 1/3 cup grated sharp Cheddar cheese

Peel and cut potatoes into small cubes. Put in a large saucepan. Cover with boiling salted water. Cook slowly, covered, until potatoes are tender, about 15 minutes. Transfer potatoes to a large bowl; mash; add milk and 2 tablespoons butter. Season with salt and pepper. Mix well. Put cabbage in potato liquid; cook until tender but crisp, about 7 minutes. Transfer to potato mixture. Mix well.

Sauté onion in 1 tablespoon melted butter in a small skillet until tender. Add to vegetables. Mix in chives or parsley. Spoon into a shallow baking dish. Sprinkle the top with cheese. Brown under a hot broiler until cheese melts and top is golden. Or bake in a preheated 450° oven about 12 minutes.

Crowdie Tatties

These mashed potatoes are flavored with a kind of Scottish soft cheese called crowdie.

Serves 4 to 6

>*⅓ cup rolled oats*
>*6 green onions, with some tops, chopped*
>*3 tablespoons butter*
>*2 cups warm mashed potatoes*
>*1 cup crowdie or drained cottage cheese*
>*¼ cup chopped fresh parsley*
>*Salt, pepper to taste*

Toast oats in a small dry skillet over medium heat until lightly browned, about 3 minutes. Remove from heat; set aside.

Sauté chopped onions in 2 tablespoons melted butter in a small skillet until tender. Turn into a medium bowl. Add mashed potatoes, crowdie or cheese, and parsley. Season with salt and pepper. Spoon into a shallow baking dish. Sprinkle the top with toasted oats. Dot with remaining 1 tablespoon butter. Bake in a preheated 375° oven about 25 minutes, or until hot and bubbly.

Kailkenney

Kail, as the Scots call their dark green curly kale, is a treasured staple vegetable. Generally it is boiled and seasoned with butter, salt and pepper, or combined with mashed boiled potatoes, onions and milk. Kail is also the common name for greens and broth and at one time was the term for a meal. "Will ye come and tak' your kail wi' me?" was once an invitation for dinner.

Serves 4

½ cup rolled oats
1 pound small, tender kale, washed
½ cup chopped green onions, with some tops
4 tablespoons butter
½ cup meat broth or water
Salt, pepper to taste
¼ cup light cream
⅛ teaspoon freshly grated nutmeg

Toast oats in a small dry skillet over medium heat until lightly browned, about 3 minutes. Remove from heat; set aside.

Strip kale leaves from their stems; cut into fine slivers. Sauté green onions in 2 tablespoons melted butter in a large saucepan until tender. Add kale and broth or water. Season with salt and pepper. Cook over moderate heat, covered, about 12 minutes, until just tender. Add cream, nutmeg, 2 tablespoons butter and toasted oats. Mix well. Cook 1 or 2 minutes.

Neep Purry

In Gaelic *neep* is the word for turnip as well as a disagreeable person. Scots are partial to the root vegetable called rutabaga, or yellow turnip, that has an appealing sweet yellow flesh. "Bashed" neeps are served with haggis. Purry derives from the French *purée*. This ginger-flavored dish is an old-time favorite.

Serves 4

 2 *pounds rutabaga*
 Salt
 ¼ cup butter
 1 tablespoon light cream
 ¼ teaspoon ground ginger
 Pepper to taste

Scrub rutabaga well and cut off outer skin. Cut into cubes. Cook, covered, in 1 inch boiling salted water about 20 minutes, until tender. Drain; turn into a serving dish; mash. Add butter, cream and ginger. Season with salt and pepper. Mash again. Serve at once.

Skirlie Tomatoes

Skirlie, or skirl-in-the-pan, is an old Scots oatmeal stuffing that has an appealing nutty flavor. Once it was served as an inexpensive meal with "chappit tatties" (mashed potatoes) and a glass of cold buttermilk. The name comes from the frizzling sound made by suet or fat frying in a skillet.

Serves 6

> 6 medium ripe tomatoes, peeled
> 2 cups finely chopped onions
> ½ cup butter
> 2 cups rolled oats
> ¼ cup chopped fresh parsley
> Salt, pepper to taste

Cut a thin slice from the top of each tomato; scoop out pulp. Invert to drain.

Sauté onions in melted butter in a large skillet until tender. Add oats; cook slowly, stirring often, until butter is absorbed, about 10 minutes. Stir in parsley. Season with salt and pepper. Spoon mixture into tomatoes, dividing evenly. Serve cold or bake in a preheated 375° oven 30 minutes.

Cauliflower Slaw

This colorful and crunchy salad goes well with poultry and game.

Serves 4 to 6

> *1 medium head (about 1½ pounds) cauliflower*
> *2 large carrots, scraped*
> *½ cup chopped green onions, with some tops*
> *½ cup chopped fresh parsley*
> *⅓ cup vegetable oil*
> *3 tablespoons cider vinegar*
> *¼ teaspoon dry mustard*
> *¼ teaspoon curry powder*
> *Salt, pepper to taste*

Wash cauliflower; remove and discard outside leaves. Break into small flowerets; slice each one thinly. Quarter carrots; slice thinly. Combine cauliflower and carrots with green onions and parsley in a large bowl.

Combine remaining ingredients and pour over vegetables. Refrigerate, covered with plastic wrap, at least 1 hour before serving.

Bannocks, Scones and Breads

The art of baking is the glory of the Scottish kitchen. "Every Scotswoman is born with a rolling pin under her arm," proclaimed an early food writer. Breadmaking in the home is still important.

Making Scottish breads is not a complicated process, and many of them can be prepared with little effort in no time at all. The mouth-watering treats range from light yeast buns and tender scones to wholesome oaten loaves and oatcakes.

Typical Scottish bread originated as a bannock, an unleavened round, flat cake that was cooked on a bakestone. Later, a variety of breads were baked on a "girdle," or griddle, one of the world's oldest cooking utensils that was brought to Scotland by the early Celts. Over the years other breads, some soft and quite thick and baked in the oven, would be called bannocks.

Through generations of baking in both the home and the shop, the appeal of old-time, high-quality products, made with respect for tradition, has persisted.

Golden Bannock

This whole wheat and cornmeal bannock is an adaptation of a Hebridean island harvest bread.

Makes one 8-inch round loaf

1 cup whole wheat flour

1 cup yellow cornmeal

2 tablespoons sugar

1 tablespoon baking powder

½ teaspoon baking soda

¾ teaspoon salt

3 tablespoons solid vegetable shortening

1 cup buttermilk

Combine flour, cornmeal, sugar, baking powder and soda, and salt in a large bowl. With a pastry blender, cut in shortening until mixture is like fine crumbs. Gradually add buttermilk, stirring, until dry ingredients are moistened. Gather into a ball.

Place in center of a lightly floured baking sheet. With floured hands, shape into an 8-inch round loaf about ½-inch thick. With a floured sharp knife, cut a large deep cross on top of loaf.

Bake in a preheated 400° oven 35 minutes, or until evenly golden and tester inserted into center comes out clean. Remove to a wire rack. Serve warm or slightly cooked, with butter and honey.

Nova Scotian
Bannock Squares

This version of the traditional bannock is made into light and crunchy sweet squares. It is from the small island of Cape Breton in Nova Scotia, sometimes called Canada's Scotland.

Makes 24 squares

> ½ cup (1 stick) butter, softened
> ½ cup light brown sugar, firmly packed
> 1 large egg
> 2 cups all-purpose flour
> 1 tablespoon baking powder
> ½ teaspoon baking soda
> ¾ teaspoon salt
> 1 cup rolled oats
> 1 cup milk

Cream butter and sugar in a large bowl until light and fluffy. Add egg; mix well.

Combine flour, baking powder and soda, and salt in à medium bowl. Stir in oats. Add to butter mixture alternately with milk, mixing until well blended. Turn batter into a greased 13 × 9 × 2-inch rectangular baking pan. Bake in a preheated 375° oven 40 minutes, or until golden brown and tester inserted into center comes out clean. Remove from oven. Cool in pan 10 minutes. Cut into squares. Serve warm or cool, plain or with butter and honey.

Midlothian Oatcakes

A crunchy, biscuit-like roundel with a pleasant nutty taste, the oatcake is a favorite Scottish bread made in many varieties. These round oatcakes include both white flour and oats. While they are not exactly like the traditional Highland oatcakes, they taste good and are rewarding to make. They are favorites around Edinburgh and in the Lothians, especially at tea time.

Makes about 10 rounds

> 1½ cups rolled oats
> ½ cup all-purpose flour
> ½ teaspoon baking powder
> ¼ teaspoon salt
> 2 tablespoons lard or solid vegetable shortening
> About 5 tablespoons hot water

Place oats in a blender or food processor. Cover; blend about 1 minute, stopping blender occasionally to stir oats, until a fine flour forms.

Thoroughly combine flour, baking powder, salt and 1¼ cups ground oats in a medium bowl. Set aside remaining ground oats.

Melt lard or shortening and, while warm, mix with 5 tablespoons hot water. Make a well in center of dry ingredients. Quickly pour in hot water mixture, stirring to make a stiff dough, adding more water if needed to make the mixture stick together. Gather into a ball.

Place on a flat surface lightly sprinkled with some of the reserved ground oats. Knead quickly and thoroughly. Quickly roll into a round about 9 inches with a ⅛-inch thickness, or as thin as possible. Pinch any edges of dough together if they split. Sprinkle top with remaining ground oats. With a floured cutter, cut into 2½-inch rounds. Transfer to an ungreased baking sheet. Bake in a preheated

350° oven about 25 minutes, until dry and firm. Remove to a wire rack. Serve warm with butter, marmalade or lemon curd. Or cool and store in an airtight container. These will keep a month or more.

Carolinian Oatcake Squares

These are sweet cookie-like oatcakes from North Carolina's western high country where many Scots live and celebrate at the Grandfather Mountain Highland Games at MacRae Meadow near Linville.

Makes 32 squares

> *1½ cups all-purpose flour*
> *½ cup sugar*
> *1 teaspoon baking powder*
> *½ teaspoon baking soda*
> *½ teaspoon salt*
> *2 cups rolled oats*
> *¾ cup vegetable shortening*
> *About 4 tablespoons cold water*

Combine flour, sugar, baking powder and soda, and salt in a large bowl. Stir in oats. With a pastry blender, cut in shortening until mixture is like fine crumbs. Add water, 1 tablespoon at a time, enough to make a stiff dough. Gather into a ball.

Turn out on a lightly floured surface. Cut into 2 parts. With a floured rolling pin, roll each part into an 8-inch square with a quarter-inch thickness. With a floured knife, cut each square into 16 two-inch squares. Place on ungreased baking sheets, about 1 inch apart.

Bake in a preheated 375° oven about 18 minutes, until golden brown and firm. Remove to a wire rack. Serve warm. Or cool and store in an airtight container.

Afternoon Tea Scones

Scones are delicious rich and crumbly biscuit-like cakes that are eaten for breakfast, with afternoon tea, or as snacks. Scots pronounce scone "skonn" (to rhyme with on). These round ones are studded with tiny, dried black currants or raisins, a favorite baking fruit.

Makes 12 rounds

> 2 cups all-purpose flour
> 2 tablespoons sugar
> 1 tablespoon baking powder
> ½ teaspoon salt
> ¼ cup (½ stick) butter, cool and diced
> ½ cup dried black currants or seedless raisins
> 1 large egg
> About ½ cup light cream
> Milk, butter and sugar for topping

Combine flour, sugar, baking powder and salt in a large bowl. With a pastry blender, cut in butter until mixture is like fine crumbs. Stir in currants.

Whisk egg and ½ cup cream in a small dish. Add to flour-butter mixture. Stir quickly and briefly to make a soft and sticky dough, adding a little more cream, if necessary. Gather into a ball. Place on a lightly floured surface. With floured hands, knead gently. Roll into a circle to a ½-inch thickness. With a floured 2½-inch round cutter, cut into rounds, leaving as little dough as possible for rerolling. Place on an ungreased baking sheet, about 1 inch apart. Brush tops lightly with milk.

Bake in a preheated 425° oven about 12 minutes, or until golden and puffed. Remove to a wire rack. Brush tops with butter and sprinkle with sugar. Allow to cool slightly, about 5 minutes. Serve warm with butter and jam or marmalade.

Raisin-Oat Scones

These small triangles have an appealing crisp texture.

Makes 12 triangles

> 1 cup all-purpose flour
> 2 tablespoons light brown sugar
> 1 tablespoon baking powder
> ½ teaspoon salt
> 1 cup rolled oats
> ¼ cup (½ stick) butter, cool and diced
> ½ cup golden raisins
> ½ cup milk

Combine flour, sugar, baking powder and salt in a large bowl. Stir in oats. With a pastry blender, cut in butter until mixture is like fine crumbs. Stir in raisins. Add milk. Stir quickly to make a soft and sticky dough. Gather into a ball.

Place on a lightly floured surface. With floured hands, knead gently. Roll into a circle to a ½-inch thickness. With a floured sharp knife, cut into 12 equal-size triangles. Place on an ungreased baking sheet, about 1 inch apart.

Bake in a preheated 425° oven for about 12 minutes, or until golden and puffed. Remove from oven to a wire rack. Allow to cool slightly, about 5 minutes. Serve warm.

Fatty Cutties

These currant-stuffed rich triangles are similar to the English Singin' Hinnies, which have so much fat in them that they sizzle or "sing" as they cook on a griddle. They have an appealing crunchy texture.

Makes 16 triangles

> *1½ cups all-purpose flour*
> *1 teaspoon baking powder*
> *¼ cup sugar*
> *½ teaspoon salt*
> *½ cup (1 stick) butter, cool and diced*
> *½ cup dried black currants or seedless raisins*
> *3 tablespoons light cream*
> *Butter for frying*

Combine flour, baking powder, sugar and salt in a large bowl. With a pastry blender, cut in butter until mixture is like fine crumbs. Stir in currants or raisins. Add cream, stirring to make a firm dough. Gather into a ball.

Place on a lightly floured surface. Cut into 2 parts. Roll each part into a circle with a ⅛-inch thickness. Cut into 8 triangles. With a spatula, gently place several of the triangles on a buttered hot griddle or in a heavy skillet. Cook over medium-high heat 2 to 3 minutes, until bottoms are golden brown. Carefully turn and cook until other sides are golden brown. Remove to a plate. Keep warm in a clean cloth while cooking the others. Serve warm, spread with butter and sprinkled with sugar if desired.

Caraway Soda Bread

These delectable round loaves of soda bread are enjoyed for breakfast or high tea. Buttermilk is the traditional liquid. This crusty bread is flavored with oval-shaped brown caraway seeds that the Scots use to impart an aromatic flavor to many baked goods.

Makes one 8-inch loaf

> 2 cups whole wheat flour
> 1 cup all-purpose flour
> 2 tablespoons light brown sugar
> 2 teaspoons baking powder
> 1 teaspoon baking soda
> ¾ teaspoon salt
> ¼ cup (½ stick) butter, cool and diced
> 2 tablespoons caraway seeds
> 1½ cups buttermilk
> Additional flour

Combine flours, sugar, baking powder and soda, and salt in a large bowl. With a pastry blender, cut in butter until mixture is like fine crumbs. Stir in caraway seeds. Make a well in center of ingredients. Gradually pour in buttermilk, stirring only until dry ingredients are moistened. Gather into a ball.

Place on a lightly floured surface. With floured hands, knead lightly and quickly until smooth. Shape into a ball. Place in center of a lightly greased baking sheet. Form into an 8-inch round with a slightly raised center. With a floured sharp knife, cut a large deep cross on top of loaf.

Bake in a preheated 375° oven for about 40 minutes, or until loaf is golden brown and sounds hollow when tapped. Remove to a wire rack. Eat warm or slightly cooled.

Aberdeen Softies

Flaky and golden, these soft biscuits are made with buttermilk and a combination of butter and shortening, which makes them very tender.

Makes 12

> 2 cups all-purpose flour
>
> 1 tablespoon sugar
>
> 2 teaspoons baking powder
>
> 1/2 teaspoon baking soda
>
> 1 teaspoon salt
>
> 3 tablespoons butter, cool and diced
>
> 2 tablespoons solid vegetable shortening
>
> 1 large egg
>
> About 1/2 cup buttermilk
>
> 2 tablespoons butter, melted

Combine flour, sugar, baking powder and soda, and salt in a large bowl. With a pastry blender, cut in butter and shortening until mixture is like fine crumbs. Whisk egg and buttermilk in a small dish. Add to flour-butter mixture. Stir quickly and briefly to make a light and soft dough, adding a little more buttermilk if necessary. Gather into a ball.

Place on a lightly floured surface. With floured hands, knead gently. Roll or pat into a circle with a 1/2-inch thickness. With a floured 2 1/2-inch round cutter, cut into rounds, leaving as little dough as possible for rerolling. Place on an ungreased baking sheet, about 1 inch apart. Brush with melted butter. Bake in a preheated 450° oven about 12 minutes, or until golden and puffed. Remove to a wire rack. Serve warm with butter.

Scots Crumpets

These delectable thin pancakes resemble the well-known English crumpets only in name. Also called Scotch or tea pancakes, they are favorites for afternoon tea as well as dessert.

Makes about 18

> 2 large eggs, separated
> 1 cup milk
> 2 tablespoons sugar
> 2 tablespoons butter, melted
> 1 cup all-purpose flour
> ¼ teaspoon salt
> ⅛ teaspoon ground allspice
> Butter for frying

Whisk egg yolks and milk in a large bowl. Add sugar and butter; mix well. Gradually sift in flour, salt and allspice, stirring as adding to thoroughly blend the ingredients.

Beat egg whites in a separate bowl until stiff; fold into batter.

To cook, for each pancake pour about 2 tablespoons batter all at once onto a well-buttered hot griddle or into a 7- or 8-inch skillet. Cook until bubbles form on the pancake surface and the underside is light golden brown, about 3 minutes. With a spatula, turn and cook until golden brown on other side. Slip onto a warm plate and keep warm in a preheated 250° oven while cooking remaining pancakes.

To serve, spread each one with a little butter, sprinkle with sugar and, if desired, a little ground cinnamon. Roll up and serve at once.

Buttermilk-Oaten Bread

This is a raisin-studded farmhouse loaf that can be used to make sandwiches or eaten as a snack.

Makes 1 loaf

>   2 cups all-purpose flour
>   3 tablespoons light brown sugar
>   1 tablespoon baking powder
>   ½ teaspoon baking soda
>   ½ teaspoon salt
>   1 cup rolled oats
>   ½ cup seedless raisins
>   2 tablespoons dark molasses
>   3 tablespoons butter, melted and cooled
>   1½ cups buttermilk

Combine flour, brown sugar, baking powder and soda, and salt in a large bowl. Stir in oats and raisins; mix well.

Combine molasses, butter and buttermilk in a small bowl. Add to dry ingredients, stirring only until they are just moistened but combined thoroughly. Turn batter into a greased 9×5×3-inch loaf pan.

Bake in a preheated 350° oven for 1 hour, or until loaf is golden brown and pick inserted into center comes out clean. Cool in pan 10 minutes. Remove from pan; cool on wire rack.

Baps

Baps, the traditional morning rolls of Scotland are soft, puffed up and floury, delicious eaten hot from the oven. They are usually made in an oval shape and have an impression in the middle of them.

Makes 20 rolls

About 3¼ cups all-purpose flour
1 envelope (1 tablespoon) active dry yeast
1 tablespoon sugar
1 teaspoon salt
¾ cup milk
½ cup water
¼ cup butter, cut in small pieces
Milk and flour for topping

Combine 1 cup flour and yeast in a large bowl. Combine sugar, salt, milk, water and butter in a small saucepan; heat only until warm, stirring to blend. Add to flour mixture. Beat with electric mixer or by hand. Add 1 cup flour; beat again. Add remaining flour, enough to make a thick soft dough; beat until smooth. Form into a ball.

Put in a large greased bowl, turning to coat entire surface. Cover with plastic wrap and put in a warm place (80° to 85°) about 1 hour, or until doubled. Turn out on a lightly floured surface. Knead until soft and elastic. Divide dough into 20 equal pieces. Shape each piece into a 3-by-1-inch oval. Place on a greased baking sheet. Brush with milk. Cover with plastic wrap and put in a warm place to rise about 30 minutes, or until doubled. Moisten a thumb and press down in center of each oval. Brush tops with milk and dust lightly with flour. Bake in a preheated 400° oven until tops are golden brown and bases are firm. Remove to wire racks for 5 minutes. Serve warm with butter.

Oat Bran Muffins

Oat bran, America's glamorous health food, is a favorite ingredient for muffins. Everybody seems to want a good recipe for them. This is one I created.

Makes 12

>   1 cup oat bran
>   1/4 cup whole wheat flour
>   1 cup rolled oats
>   2 teaspoons baking powder
>   1/2 teaspoon baking soda
>   1/2 teaspoon salt
>   1/2 cup seedless raisins
>   2 tablespoons vegetable oil
>   1/4 cup honey
>   1 egg white
>   1 cup buttermilk

Combine oat bran, flour, oats, baking powder and soda, and salt in a large bowl. Stir in raisins.

Whisk oil, honey, egg white and buttermilk in a small bowl. Add to dry ingredients, stirring until just moistened. Spoon into 12 2½-inch greased muffin-pan cups, filling two-thirds full. Bake in a preheated 425° oven 15 to 17 minutes, until golden brown and pick inserted into center comes out clean. Remove muffins immediately from cups, transferring to a wire rack. Serve warm or cool.

Shortbread, Cookies and Cakes

Scots enjoy their characteristic shortbreads, cookies (called biscuits) and cakes with afternoon tea, for all special and family celebrations and often as symbols of hospitality or "welcomes" for neighbors and friends.

Cakes were originally sweetened doughs enhanced with dried fruits and spices. Many were like breads and the words became confused because of the similarity of the ingredients. Even biscuits were sometimes called "bisk-cakes." As flavorings for these treats Scots use such spices as pungent ginger and cinnamon, caraway seeds, currants, nuts, lemon juice and rind, almond extract, molasses or syrup, and especially clover and heather honey, esteemed as among the best in the world.

Baked specialties had symbolic or religious significance in early Scotland and were served for seasonal festivals as well as weddings and birthdays.

No Scottish celebration of the Christmas season is complete without their famous shortbread and Dundee Cake. Black Bun, also called "sweetie loaf," a dark rich fruitcake baked in pastry, is a favorite New Year's Eve or Hogmanay specialty. Originally it was a Twelfth Night plum cake. Basic ingredients are raisins, currants, almonds, several spices, shortening, sugar and a liquor such as Scotch

89

whisky, brandy or sherry. The cake should be stored several weeks in a covered tin container before it is eaten so it can mature.

Praised by one poet as a "joy of our gourmand youth," Robert Louis Stevenson called the cake "a black substance inimical to life." Although some Scots prepare Black Bun with family recipes, many buy it in cans or from bakeries.

Shortbread, sometimes called Scotch cake, is a unique Scottish creation. While not a bread or a cake, it isn't quite a cookie either. Perhaps it's best described as a rich, slightly sweet cookie-type cake with a pleasing favor and texture that is crisp and somewhat crumbly.

Although there are now many kinds of shortbread, the traditional rich and "short" one is made with only flour, sugar and plenty of butter (no substitutes). It is important to use only the finest ingredients such as all-purpose flour, superfine or granulated sugar, and especially fresh butter, lightly salted or unsalted.

The preparation of shortbread requires skill and patience, for the ingredients must be perfectly blended, carefully shaped and cooked exactly. It demands hawklike attention. Purists insist that the working together of the ingredients be done by hand or with the fingertips until the particles cling together and can be shaped into a ball. The dough should be baked slowly and quite long to have a sandy hue or pale golden color but not be brown.

Shortbread can be baked in various forms—from bars and wedges to rings and squares. Some rounds of dough are shaped in a circular wooden or glazed earthenware mold that has etched designs of thistle, heather, flowers or Scottish motifs.

Regardless of the shape, all shortbreads are pricked over the top with the tines of a fork before being baked. This is to prevent the dough from blistering. Some are also notched or pinched around the edges.

Shortbread is enjoyed the year round and for all Scottish celebrations. It goes well with almost anything—from whisky to ice cream.

There is nothing to compare with the wonderful aroma and flavor of home-baked shortbread.

Shortbread Fingers

This recipe is for the classic shortbread that is made in oblong shapes.

Makes about 3 dozen

> 1 cup (2 sticks) unsalted butter, softened
> 1/2 cup sugar
> 2 cups all-purpose flour
> 1/8 teaspoon salt

Cream butter with a flat wooden spoon in a large deep bowl. Add sugar gradually, beating until light and fluffy. Sift in flour, 1 cup at a time, and salt, mixing as adding. Combine thoroughly, preferably with the fingers (or a spoon) until mixture is uniformly crumbly and can be pressed together to form a ball.

Turn out dough on a lightly floured smooth, cool surface. Roll gently with a wooden rolling pin into a large rectangle about 1/2 inch thick. With a ruler mark out fingers, 2 1/2 inches long and 1 inch wide. Prick tops of each finger with tines of a fork to form 3 rows. Remove with a spatula to ungreased baking sheets, placing 1/2 inch apart. Put in a preheated 325° oven. Reduce heat at once to 275° and bake 25 to 30 minutes, or until light golden on the bottom and sandy white on top and firm to the touch. Watch carefully during the baking through the glass window on the oven door to observe the color so it does not become brown. With a spatula, remove at once to wire racks. Cool completely. Wrap in wax paper or foil or store in airtight containers. Serve sprinkled with granulated or confectioners' sugar, if desired.

Petticoat Tails

This flat round of shortbread has a central circle cut out and the rest divided into wedges to represent the skirt panels of women's petticoats of the 19th century, hence the name.

Makes 8 wedges and 1 round

> ½ cup (1 stick) butter, softened
> ¼ cup sugar
> 1 cup all-purpose flour
> ½ cup cornstarch
> ⅛ teaspoon salt
> Confectioners' sugar

Cream butter and sugar in a large bowl until light and fluffy. Gradually sift in flour, cornstarch and salt, mixing as adding. Combine thoroughly, preferably with the fingers (or a wooden spoon) until mixture is uniformly crumbly and can be pressed together to form a ball.

Place in center of a lightly floured ungreased baking sheet. Roll or pat into a circle to a ⅛-inch thickness. With a floured cookie cutter or glass, cut out a 3-inch round in the center. Do not remove. With a floured sharp knife, cut the outer circle into 8 wedges to form "petticoat tails." Prick all over the top with tines of a fork. Bake in a preheated 300° oven about 20 minutes, or until sandy white and firm to the touch. With a spatula, remove at once to a wire rack. Sprinkle with confectioners' sugar. To serve, arrange wedges around center round on a serving plate.

Ayrshire Shortbread

This is an unusual rich shortbread; it includes an egg yolk and cream. It is from the region of Ayrshire in southwestern Scotland, a rich farming area. The shortbread is made in small rounds or fancy shapes.

Makes about 35

> 1 cup (2 sticks) butter, softened
> ½ cup sugar, preferably superfine
> 2 cups all-purpose flour
> ⅛ teaspoon salt
> 1 egg yolk
> 1 tablespoon cream
> Granulated or confectioners' sugar

Cream butter with a flat wooden spoon in a large deep bowl. Add sugar gradually, beating until light and fluffy. Sift in flour, 1 cup at a time, and salt, mixing as adding. Make a well in the center; add egg yolk and cream. Combine thoroughly until mixture can be pressed together to form a ball.

Turn out dough on a lightly floured smooth, cool surface. Roll gently with a wooden rolling pin to ¼-inch thickness, keeping the shape as circular as possible. With a floured cutter, cut into 2½-inch circles. Prick tops of each circle with tines of a fork. With a spatula, transfer to an ungreased baking sheet, placing ½ inch apart. Bake in a preheated 300° oven 10 to 12 minutes, until pale golden and firm to the touch. With a spatula, remove carefully at once to wire racks to cool completely. While still warm, sprinkle with sugar.

Tantallon Cakes

This is an appealing lemon-flavored short-bread cookie. It is named for Tantallon Castle, a dramatic rose-colored ruined stronghold a few miles east of North Berwick, now a national monument.

Makes about 16 cookies

> *½ cup (1 stick) butter, softened*
> *⅓ cup sugar, preferably superfine*
> *1 teaspoon grated lemon rind*
> *1 large egg, beaten*
> *2 tablespoons cornstarch*
> *⅛ teaspoon salt*
> *About 1¼ cups all-purpose flour*
> *Confectioners' sugar*

Cream butter with a flat wooden spoon in a large deep bowl. Add sugar gradually, beating until light and fluffy. Stir in lemon rind. Add egg; mix well. Gradually sift in cornstarch, salt and flour, ½ cup at a time, using enough flour until mixture can be pressed together to form a ball.

Turn out dough on a lightly floured smooth, cool surface. Gently roll out with a wooden rolling pin to ¼-inch thickness, keeping the shape as circular as possible. With a floured cutter, cut into 2½-inch circles. Prick tops of each circle all over with a fork. With a spatula, remove to an ungreased baking sheet, placing ½ inches apart. Bake in a preheated 325° oven 12 to 15 minutes, or until pale golden and firm to the touch. With a spatula, remove at once to a wire rack to cool completely. Sprinkle with confectioners' sugar.

Melting Moments

These delicate teatime cookies are so tender that they practically melt in the mouth.

Makes 3 dozen

> ¾ cup (1½ sticks) butter, softened
> ½ cup sugar
> 1 teaspoon grated lemon rind
> 2 cups cornstarch
> 1 teaspoon baking powder
> 2 large eggs, beaten
> Confectioners' sugar

Cream butter and sugar in a large bowl until light and fluffy. Stir in lemon rind. Sift in cornstarch and baking powder, adding a little at a time alternately with beaten eggs, mixing well after each addition to make a light and creamy batter.

Spoon by large spoonfuls into buttered miniature muffin pans. Bake in a preheated 425° oven about 12 minutes, until a pick inserted into center comes out clean and tops are a delicate golden color. With a knife, carefully remove to a wire rack. Cool. Serve sprinkled with confectioners' sugar.

Rock Buns

Flavored with spices and currants, these small cakes are rocky-looking mounds with a crusty exterior and soft center. They have a pleasing taste and good keeping quality.

Makes about 3 dozen

> 2 cups all-purpose flour
> 3 tablespoons sugar
> 1½ teaspoons baking powder
> ¼ teaspoon ground cinnamon
> ⅛ teaspoon ground nutmeg
> ⅛ teaspoon ground cloves
> ½ teaspoon salt
> ½ cup (1 stick) butter, cool and diced
> ½ cup dried black currants or seedless raisins
> 1 large egg
> About ½ cup milk

Sift flour, sugar, baking powder, cinnamon, nutmeg, cloves and salt into a large bowl. With a pastry blender, cut in butter until mixture is like fine crumbs. Stir in currants or raisins.

Whisk egg and ½ cup milk in a small dish. Add to flour-butter mixture; mix well to make a stiff dough, adding a little more milk if necessary. Drop by tablespoonfuls on greased cookie sheets, about 1 inch apart.

Bake in a preheated 400° oven 15 minutes, until a pick inserted into center comes out clean. Transfer to wire racks. Serve warm, split and spread with butter. Or cool and store in airtight containers.

Oaties

These are crunchy oat-molasses squares.

Makes 16

    ¼ cup molasses
    ½ cup (1 stick) butter, cut in small pieces
    ¼ cup sugar
    1 cup all-purpose flour
    1 teaspoon baking powder
    ½ teaspoon baking soda
    ½ teaspoon salt
    1 cup rolled oats
    Additional 3 tablespoons rolled oats

Combine molasses, butter and sugar in a small saucepan. Heat, stirring occasionally, until butter melts. Remove from heat.

Sift flour, baking powder and soda, and salt into a large bowl. Stir in 1 cup oats. Add molasses-butter mixture; mix well. Turn into a greased 9 × 9 × 2-inch baking pan, spreading evenly. Sprinkle top with additional oats. Bake in a preheated 375° oven 20 minutes, until golden and firm. Cut into squares. Cool in pan 10 minutes. Remove to a wire rack. Cool.

Seed Cake

This old-time tea cake is flavored with spicy, pungent caraway seeds and nutmeg. Scots enjoy it on Handsel Monday, the first Monday of the New Year.

Makes 1 loaf

½ cup (1 stick) butter, softened

½ cup sugar

3 large eggs

2 cups all-purpose flour

2 teaspoons baking powder

⅛ teaspoon freshly grated nutmeg

½ teaspoon salt

1 tablespoon caraway seeds

⅓ to ½ cup milk

Cream butter and sugar in a large bowl until light and fluffy. Add eggs, one at a time, beating after each addition.

Sift flour, baking powder, nutmeg and salt into a medium bowl. Stir in caraway seeds. Add to butter-sugar mixture, alternating with enough milk to make a firm smooth batter.

Turn batter into a greased 9×5×3-inch loaf pan. Bake in a preheated 350° oven about 50 minutes, until pick inserted into center comes out clean and top is golden. Cool in pan 10 minutes. Remove from pan; cool on a wire rack. Wrap in foil. Leave in a cool, dry place up to 3 days. To serve, slice thin.

Diet Loaf

The name of this traditional sponge cake, flavored with cinnamon and lemon, is misleading. It's hardly diet fare.

Makes 1 loaf

1 cup (2 sticks) butter, softened
1 cup sugar
1 teaspoon grated lemon rind
4 large eggs
2 cups all-purpose flour
1 teaspoon baking powder
1/2 teaspoon ground cinnamon
1/4 teaspoon salt
Confectioners' sugar

Cream butter and sugar in a large bowl until light and fluffy. Stir in lemon rind. Add eggs, one at a time, beating after each addition.

Sift flour, baking powder, cinnamon and salt into a medium bowl. Add to butter-sugar mixture, beating until well blended. Turn batter into a greased 9 × 5 × 3-inch loaf pan. Bake in a preheated 350° oven 1 hour, or until pick inserted into center comes out clean and top is golden. Cool in pan 10 minutes. Remove from pan; cool on a wire rack. Wrap in foil. Leave in a cool dry place up to 3 days. To serve, sprinkle with confectioners' sugar and slice thin.

Marmalade Pudding Cake

This light pudding cake is best made with Scotch golden shred marmalade, prepared with bitter Seville oranges.

Serves 6 to 8

> 5 tablespoons butter, softened
> ½ cup sugar
> 2 large eggs
> 1 cup all-purpose flour
> 1½ teaspoons baking powder
> ¼ teaspoon baking soda
> ½ teaspoon ground cinnamon
> ¼ teaspoon salt
> ½ cup buttermilk
> 1 teaspoon grated orange rind
> ½ teaspoon vanilla extract
> 1 cup orange marmalade

With a pastry brush, coat bottom and sides of a 9 × 5 × 3-inch loaf pan with 1 tablespoon butter.

Cream 4 tablespoons butter and sugar in a large bowl until light and fluffy. Add eggs, one at a time, beating after each addition. Sift in flour, baking powder and soda, cinnamon and salt, adding alternately with buttermilk, beating until well blended. Stir in orange peel and vanilla; mix well.

Heat marmalade in a small saucepan. Pour into buttered loaf pan, spreading evenly. Add batter, spreading evenly. Bake in a preheated 350° oven about 45 minutes, until tester inserted into center comes out clean. Cool in pan 10 minutes. Run a sharp knife around the edges. Carefully invert onto a serving plate. Serve warm or cool.

Fochabers Gingerbread

Scots have dozens of recipes for gingerbread made in various forms and with a wide range of ingredients. This one includes almonds and candied fruit and is flavored with beer.

Makes 20 small squares

  1 cup (2 sticks) butter, softened
  ½ cup sugar
  ¾ cup warm dark molasses
  2 large eggs
  3½ cups all-purpose flour
  1 teaspoon baking soda
  2 teaspoons ground ginger
  1 teaspoon ground cinnamon
  ¼ teaspoon ground cloves
  ¼ teaspoon ground allspice
  ¼ teaspoon salt
  ½ cup dried black currants or seedless raisins
  ½ cup golden raisins
  ½ cup diced mixed candied fruit
  ½ cup ground blanched almonds
  1 cup beer

Cream butter and sugar in a large bowl until light and fluffy. Add warm molasses and eggs, one at a time, mixing well after each addition.

Combine flour, baking soda, ginger, cinnamon, cloves, allspice and salt in a medium bowl. Stir in currants, raisins, candied fruit and almonds. Add 1 cup at a time, alternately with beer, to butter-molasses mixture, mixing well after each addition. Mix to thoroughly combine ingredients.

Turn into a greased 13 × 9 × 2-inch baking pan, spreading evenly. Bake in a preheated 325° oven 45 to 50 minutes, until tester inserted into center comes out clean. Cool in pan on a wire rack 10 minutes. Remove from pan; cool completely on rack. Wrap in foil. Leave in a cool dry place up to 3 days. To serve, cut into squares.

Parkins

These are moist squares of oatmeal ginger-bread that are traditional fare in northern England and Scotland.

Makes one 9-inch square cake

1 cup dark molasses
½ cup sugar
½ cup (1 stick) butter, cut in small pieces
1 large egg
1 cup milk
2¼ cups all-purpose flour
2 teaspoons baking powder
1 teaspoon ground ginger
½ teaspoon ground cinnamon
½ teaspoon salt
2 cups rolled oats

Combine molasses, sugar and butter in a small saucepan. Heat, stirring occasionally, until butter melts. Remove from heat.

Whisk egg in a small dish; add milk; whisk. Gradually add to molasses mixture.

Sift flour, baking powder, ginger, cinnamon and salt into a large bowl. Gradually add molasses-milk mixture. Mix until smooth. Stir in oats; mix well.

Turn into a greased 9 × 9 × 2-inch baking pan; spread evenly. Bake in a preheated 350° oven about 40 minutes, or until pick inserted into center comes out clean. Cool in pan on a wire rack 10 minutes. Remove from pan. Cool completely on rack. Wrap in foil. To serve, cut into squares.

Dundee Cake

Scotland's famous light fruitcake, topped with a characteristic trademark, almonds, is from Dundee, an old seaport northeast of Edinburgh. A favorite tea-time treat since the 1800s, the cake is renowned throughout Britain and is exported in tins around the world. It keeps well and has an excellent flavor. Scots enjoy the butter-rich cake for all special occasions, including weddings.

Makes one 8-inch round cake

> 1 cup (2 sticks) butter, softened
> 1 cup sugar
> 5 large eggs
> 2½ cups all-purpose flour
> 1 teaspoon baking powder
> ½ teaspoon salt
> ¾ cup dried black currants
> ¾ cup golden raisins
> ½ cup diced mixed candied fruit
> ½ cup ground blanched almonds
> 1 tablespoon grated orange rind
> 28 whole blanched almonds

Cream butter and sugar in a large bowl until light and fluffy. Add eggs, one at a time, beating after each addition. Sift in flour, baking powder and salt, adding alternately with currants, raisins, candied fruit, almonds and orange rind. Mix to combine thoroughly.

Turn into a greased and floured 8-inch round cake pan. Arrange whole almonds in circles on top of cake. Bake in a preheated 300° oven 1½ hours, or until tester inserted into center comes out clean. Let cool in pan 10 minutes. Remove from pan. Put on a wire rack to cool. Wrap in foil. Leave in a cool dry place to "mellow" for a few days. Or store in an airtight container. To serve, cut into slices.

Christmas Fruit Cake

Makes one 10-inch round cake

1½ cups dried black currants
1½ cups seedless raisins
1½ cups golden raisins
2 cups diced mixed candied fruit
2 cups all-purpose flour
½ teaspoon baking powder
1 teaspoon ground cinnamon
1 teaspoon ground allspice
½ teaspoon salt
1 cup (2 sticks) butter, softened
1 cup light brown sugar, firmly packed
1 cup ground blanched almonds
4 large eggs
¼ cup Scotch whisky or brandy
¼ cup currant jelly

Combine currants, raisins, fruit and ½ cup flour in a large bowl. Mix with a fork to coat fruit. Sift remaining 1½ cups flour, baking powder, cinnamon, allspice and salt into a medium bowl.

Cream butter and sugar in a large bowl until light and fluffy. Stir in almonds. Add eggs, one at a time. Add flour mixture, ½ cup at a time. Stir in floured fruit, 1 cup at a time. Pour in Scotch or brandy. Mix well.

Line a well-buttered 10×3-inch spring-form cake pan with a buttered sheet of waxed paper. Turn in batter, spreading evenly. Bake in a 325° oven 1¾ hours, or until tester inserted into center comes out clean. Let cool in pan 30 minutes. Remove sides of pan. Remove cake from bottom of pan. Put on a wire rack to cool. Peel off paper.

Heat the jelly. Spread with a pastry brush over top and sides of cake. Wrap in foil. Leave in a cool dry place to "mellow" for a few days. Or store in an airtight container.

Desserts

There is a whimsical side to Scottish food that mocks its reputation as being wholesome and plain: Scots have a passion for all things sweet. Their desserts are luscious, ranging from filmy light creams and silken-smooth custards to elaborate puddings and pastries.

The oldest Scottish desserts were puddings made with grains and fruit, sweetened with honey. Over the years the Scots created so many imaginative "sweet things," as they called desserts, that they became known as "pudding lovers." F. Marian McNeil refers to a lady's cook "who could make so many puddings, 99 if I remember right."

One of the most beloved desserts is a steamed pudding called Clootie Dumplin'. It is served for family celebrations, especially children's birthdays, and, in the Highlands, as a New Year's treat. Rich and sweet, it was made originally with oatmeal and suet. Now it includes flour and butter, mixed dried fruit, brown sugar, eggs, syrup or molasses and spices. Also called Cloutie Puddin' or Fruit Dumplin', it is wrapped and boiled in a "cloute" or "clottie," the Scottish word for cloth.

The pudding is served hot as it is turned out of the cloth with cream or a sweet sauce. Or it can be served sliced, buttered, sprinkled with sugar and enjoyed with tea. The cold slices can also be fried in butter and served for breakfast with eggs, bacon or sausage.

Many Scots prepare the pudding with family recipes or purchase it at bakeries. In Scotland a great place to enjoy the dessert is The Three Rowans Restaurant on the Isle of Skye where they have a Folk and Clootie Dumpling Evening.

Among the treasured array of cold sweets are those made with cream, eggs and flavorings as well as a generous lacing of spirits. In his novel *The Bride of Lammermoor* Sir Walter Scott describes a dinner with desserts that were "a fairy feast of cream, jellies, strawberries, sweetmeats, almond-cream and lemon-cream."

Cranachan

Scotland's national pudding—called cranachan or crowdie cream—is a pleasing combination of toasted oats, whipped cream and Scotch whisky. Many recipes also include fresh berries in season.

Serves 4

> *½ cup rolled oats*
>
> *1 cup heavy cream, chilled*
>
> *2 tablespoons sugar, preferably superfine*
>
> *2 tablespoons Scotch whisky*
>
> *2 cups fresh blueberries or other berries*

Spread oats in a shallow baking pan. Toast in a preheated 375° oven, shaking occasionally, about 12 minutes or until light golden brown. Remove from oven. Cool.

Whip cream in a chilled large bowl until soft peaks form; add sugar and whisky gradually. Whip until mixture thickens. Fold in toasted oats.

Layer cream mixture and berries in 4 tall stemmed dessert glasses, beginning with a layer of cream and topping with a layer of berries. Refrigerate up to 2 hours.

Sky Mist

This is another version of cranachan. To prepare, follow instructions for cranachan but substitute Drambuie for Scotch whisky and use small strawberries or quartered whole ones.

Caledonian Cream

This traditional cream dessert is flavored with orange marmalade and Drambuie.

Serves 6

> *½ cup orange marmalade*
>
> *3 tablespoons Drambuie*
>
> *2 teaspoons fresh lemon juice*
>
> *2 cups heavy cream, chilled*
>
> *3 tablespoons confectioners' sugar*

Combine marmalade, Drambuie and lemon juice in a small dish. Leave at room temperature 30 minutes.

Whip cream in a chilled large bowl until soft peaks form; gradually add sugar. Whip until mixture thickens. Fold in marmalade mixture. Spoon mixture into 6 stemmed dessert glasses, dividing equally. Garnish tops with a bit of orange peel from marmalade, if desired. Refrigerate up to 2 hours.

Whim Wham

Who knows when this dessert was created? But Scott mentioned "whim whams" in one of his novels.

Serves 6

> 12 lady fingers, split in halves
> About 1 cup red currant or raspberry jelly
> 2 cups heavy cream, chilled
> ¼ cup sugar, preferably superfine
> ½ teaspoon grated lemon rind
> ⅓ cup dry white wine

Spread one side of each lady finger half with jelly; set aside.

Whip cream in a chilled large bowl until soft peaks form; gradually add sugar, lemon rind and wine. Whip until mixture thickens.

Arrange a layer of 8 lady finger halves, jelly sides up, in a shallow serving dish. Top with a layer of the whipped cream mixture. Repeat with 2 more layers of lady fingers and cream. Garnish the top with bits of jelly. Refrigerate up to 2 hours before serving.

Edinburgh Fog

This attractive cream, also called Edinburgh Mist, is made traditionally with vanilla-flavored whipped cream, toasted almonds and crushed ratafia biscuits (small almond-flavored macaroons that were once very popular and now sold in confectioners').

Serves 6

> ½ cup chopped blanched almonds
> 2 cups heavy cream, chilled
> 3 tablespoons sugar, preferably superfine
> 1 tablespoon dry sherry
> 1 teaspoon vanilla extract
> 2 cups crumbled almond macaroons

Put almonds in a shallow baking pan. Toast in a preheated 325° oven, stirring occasionally, about 10 minutes, until light golden brown.

Whip cream in a chilled large bowl until soft peaks form; gradually add sugar, sherry and vanilla. Whip until mixture thickens. Fold in macaroons. Spoon mixture into 6 stemmed dessert glasses, dividing equally. Sprinkle tops with toasted almonds. Refrigerate up to 2 hours before serving.

Everlasting Syllabub

This frothy liquorous cream, called syllabub or sillyboo, has long been a favorite Scottish company dessert. The name derives from a wine that once came from Sillery in the Champagne region of France, and bub is slang for a bubbling drink.

Serves 6

> *Grated rind and juice of 1 large lemon*
> *½ cup dry white wine*
> *¼ cup brandy*
> *2 cups heavy cream, chilled*
> *¼ cup sugar, preferably superfine*
> *Freshly grated nutmeg*

Combine lemon rind and juice, wine and brandy in a small dish. Leave at room temperature 1 hour to blend flavors; strain.

Whip cream in a chilled large bowl until soft peaks form; gradually add sugar and wine mixture. Whip until mixture thickens. Spoon into 6 stemmed dessert glasses, dividing equally. Garnish tops with a little grated nutmeg. Serve at once or refrigerate up to 2 hours.

Scottish Islands

In Scotland the classic dessert called Floating Islands is made with puffs of pink meringue resting on wine-flavored whipped cream.

Serves 8

> 3 egg whites
> 6 tablespoons sugar
> Pinch salt
> 1/3 cup red currant or raspberry jelly
> 1 1/2 cups heavy cream, chilled
> 1 teaspoon grated lemon rind
> 1/4 cup ruby port or sherry

Beat egg whites in a large bowl until foamy; gradually add 3 tablespoons sugar and salt, beating as adding until stiff. Fold in jelly.

Meanwhile, whip cream in a chilled large bowl until soft peaks form. Gradually beat in remaining 3 tablespoons sugar, beating as adding, until mixture thickens. Fold in lemon rind and port or sherry. Spoon into a shallow glass bowl or serving dish. Top with large spoonfuls of beaten egg whites to form "islands" on top. Refrigerate up to 2 hours before serving.

Atholl Brose Dessert

This pleasant honey–and whisky–flavored cream is a modern dessert that has the same name as an ancient Highland drink (page 131).

Serves 6

> 12 tablespoons rolled oats
> ½ cup Scotch whisky
> ½ cup honey, preferably heather
> 2 cups heavy cream, chilled
> 2 tablespoons confectioners' sugar
> ⅛ teaspoon freshly grated nutmeg
> 1½ cups sliced fresh ripe strawberries
> 6 whole fresh ripe strawberries, hulled

Spread oats in a shallow baking pan. Toast in a preheated 375° oven, shaking occasionally, about 12 minutes, until light golden brown. Remove from oven. Cool.

Combine whisky and honey in a small dish. Leave at room temperature up to 1 hour.

Whip cream in a chilled large bowl until soft peaks form; gradually add whisky mixture, sugar and nutmeg. Whip until mixture thickens.

Layer ¼ cup sliced strawberries, 1 tablespoon toasted oats and ⅙ whipped cream mixture in 6 stemmed dessert glasses. Garnish the top of each with a whole strawberry. Refrigerate up to 2 hours before serving.

Apple Flory

An ancestor of apple pie, this one has an unusual combination of flavors—lemon juice and rind, orange marmalade and raisins. Flory is the Scottish name for a two-crust pie.

Serves 6 to 8

> Pastry for 2-crust 9-inch pie
> 4 cups chopped peeled tart apples (about 4 medium)
> 2 tablespoons fresh lemon juice
> 1 teaspoon grated lemon rind
> 1/3 cup orange marmalade
> 1/3 cup golden raisins
> 1/2 cup firm-textured white bread crumbs
> 4 tablespoons sugar
> 4 tablespoons butter

Line a 9-inch pie pan with pastry. Combine apples, lemon juice and rind in a large bowl. Add marmalade, raisins, bread crumbs and 3 tablespoons sugar; mix well. Fill pie shell; dot top with 2 tablespoons butter. Cover with pastry; flute edges to seal; cut gashes in crust. Bake in a preheated 450° oven for 10 minutes; reduce the oven temperature to 350° and continue baking for 40 minutes, until crust is golden brown and flaky. Remove from oven and transfer to a cooling rack. Rub top with remaining 2 tablespoons butter and sprinkle with remaining 1 tablespoon sugar. Serve warm or at room temperature.

Raspberry Fool

A classic fool is a simple dessert, a purée of fresh berries or fruit folded into sweetened whipped cream; in Scotland the dessert is enhanced with a liqueur. The origin of the amusing name is not certain. At one time it was synonymous with the word trifle, meaning something of little consequence. Or, perhaps, a bit of foolishness—a mere trifle.

Scots are fond of fools made with gooseberries, tart and pale green in color with an agreeably acidic sweetness. They are also partial to those made with raspberries, such as this colorful dessert.

Serves 6

>*3 cups fresh raspberries*
>*½ cup sugar, preferably superfine*
>*3 tablespoons Drambuie*
>*1½ cups heavy cream, chilled*
>*Whole raspberries for garnish*

Purée raspberries with ¼ cup sugar in a blender or food processor. Turn into a large bowl. Stir in Drambuie.

Whip cream in a chilled large bowl until soft peaks form; gradually add remaining ¼ cup sugar. Whip until mixture thickens. Fold in raspberry purée. Spoon into a glass bowl or 6 stemmed dessert glasses, dividing equally. Garnish tops with 1 or 2 whole raspberries. Refrigerate up to 2 hours.

Blackberry Crumble

A classic dessert called a crumble is closely akin to American cobbler but has a crisp oat topping.

Serves 6

> 4 cups fresh ripe blackberries
> ¼ cup sugar
> 1 tablespoon fresh lemon juice
> ¾ cup all-purpose flour
> ¾ cup rolled oats
> ⅓ cup brown sugar
> ½ teaspoon ground cinnamon
> ½ cup (1 stick) butter, cool and diced

Put blackberries in a buttered 8- or 9-inch square baking dish. Sprinkle with sugar and lemon juice.

Combine flour, oats, brown sugar and cinnamon in a medium bowl. With a pastry blender, cut in butter until mixture is uniformly crumbly. Spread evenly over blackberries to make a topping. Bake in a preheated 375° oven about 45 minutes, or until top is golden and crisp. Serve warm or cold with heavy cream or vanilla ice cream.

Lemon Sponge

This lemony pudding-cake is a typical Scottish dessert known as a sponge. When baked, the bottom custard sauce is ladled over the cake-like topping.

Serves 4 to 6

>*1 large lemon*
>*¼ cup (½ stick) butter, softened*
>*¾ cup sugar*
>*3 large eggs, separated*
>*¼ cup all-purpose flour*
>*⅛ teaspoon salt*
>*1½ cups milk*
>*Confectioners' sugar*

Grate lemon rind; squeeze out juice. Reserve.

Cream butter and sugar in a large bowl until light and fluffy. Mix in lemon rind. Add egg yolks, one at a time; beat thoroughly. Sift in flour and salt alternately with milk and lemon juice, beating until well blended.

Beat egg whites in a large bowl until firm peaks form. Fold into batter. Turn into a buttered 1½-quart round baking dish. Set in a shallow baking pan with 2 inches hot water. Bake in a preheated 350° oven for 50 minutes, or until tester inserted into center comes out clean. Serve warm sprinkled with confectioners' sugar.

Lemon Curd

Lemon curd, also called lemon butter or lemon cheese, is a traditional British preserve made of butter, sugar and eggs and flavored with fresh lemon juice and rind. It has an appealing smooth texture and is delectably tart. The Scots eat the preserve at afternoon tea as a spread on buttered bread or toast, scones or with oatcakes. It can also be used to fill tarts, cakes and pies.

Makes about 2 cups

> 3 large lemons
> ½ cup (1 stick) butter, softened
> 1 cup sugar
> 3 large eggs
> 2 egg yolks

Wash lemons; roll on a flat surface. Squeeze and strain juice of lemons into a small dish. Grate rind of lemons; add to juice.

Melt butter in top of a double boiler over simmering water. Stir in lemon juice and rind. Gradually add sugar, stirring with a wooden spoon.

Whisk eggs and egg yolks in a small dish until light and creamy; add to butter mixture. Cook slowly, stirring almost constantly, about 15 minutes, until very thick. Do not boil, or mixture will curdle. Remove from heat; pour at once into a clean jar or container. Cover, cool, refrigerate. The curd will keep refrigerated up to 2 weeks.

Tipsy Laird

A rich cold pudding known as Tipsy Laird (Lord) or Scots trifle is a favorite holiday or company dessert that is served regally in an elegant glass bowl. In Scotland it is made traditionally with sponge cake fingers, crushed ratafia biscuits or cookies; Scotch whisky or brandy, sherry or Drambuie; a rich custard; and a topping of whipped cream. Sometimes fresh raspberries or strawberries are also included.

Serves 8

One 8 × 4 × 2-inch spongecake

¾ cup raspberry or strawberry jam

1 cup finely crumbled almond macaroons

¼ cup dry sherry or Drambuie

¼ cup Scotch whisky or brandy

Custard, chilled (recipe below)

2 cups fresh ripe raspberries or strawberries (optional)

1 cup heavy cream, chilled

3 tablespoons confectioners' sugar

½ teaspoon vanilla extract

3 tablespoons toasted blanched almond slivers

Whole fresh raspberries or strawberries, hulled

Slice spongecake crosswise into two layers. Spread the surface of one layer with jam, spreading evenly. Cut lengthwise in half; cut each half into eight 1-inch fingers. Arrange fingers in a trifle dish or glass serving bowl. Sprinkle with crumbled macaroons. Combine sherry or Drambuie and whisky or brandy; pour over fingers and let soak in. Then top with chilled custard sauce. Place in refrigerator until custard is partially absorbed by the cake, 1 hour or longer. Top with berries.

Whip cream in a chilled large bowl until soft peaks form. Add confectioners' sugar and vanilla gradually. Whip until mixture thickens. Spread over custard in swirls. Garnish top with toasted almonds and whole berries. Serve at once or refrigerate up to 2 hours before serving.

Custard

> 4 large egg yolks
> ⅓ cup sugar
> ⅛ teaspoon salt
> 1½ cups milk, scalded
> ½ teaspoon vanilla extract

Combine egg yolks, sugar and salt in top of a double boiler. Whisk vigorously. Slowly stir in warm scalded milk. Cook over simmering, not boiling, water, stirring constantly until mixture thickens and coats the spoon, about 7 minutes. Remove pan from hot water and place in a pan of cold water to cool. Stir in vanilla. Refrigerate, covered with plastic wrap, to chill.

Traditional Foods, With and Without Oats

Dishes With Oats

Oats have sustained Scots for centuries. They are the most nutritious of grains and an excellent energy food. "Oatmeal cakes and oatmeal porridge have made Scotchmen," is a popular saying. The well-developed large physiques of the Scots have been credited to their oat diet. It is also believed that the "Scottish genius takes its fire from the phosphorous of oatmeal."

Oats are a wholegrain. Each hulled oat (or groat, as it is called) still contains its original bran, germ and endosperm. The most common form of oats, rolled oats, are so-called because the whole groats are steamed and then flattened between rollers before being made into flakes. They are made in three thicknesses. The two most widely available in American stores are regular (also called old-fashioned) and quick-cooking. Both have the same nutritional benefits and can be used interchangeably. Scotch or steel-cut oats (called pinhead in Scotland) are cut with stone rather than steel rollers and are nuttier, chewier and more coarsely ground. They are sold in specialty or health food stores.

When Scots mention oatmeal, they mean the milled grain. They use fine, medium and coarse oatmeal for various dishes. In America oats are popularly called oatmeal—a catchall term for various kinds of oats and popular breakfast cereals such as porridge.

Porridge

Porridge is a beloved Scottish hot breakfast dish. The preparation and serving of "the halesome parritch, Chief of Scotia's food," as Robbie Burns called it, has considerable tradition and ritual.

For porridge oats, Scots use milled (a more coarsely ground product) rather than rolled oats. Their milled oats are sold in American stores as Scotch or Irish oatmeal. Scottish-style porridge oats, made and sold in the United States, are extra thick rolled oats. All should be prepared according to the package instructions.

As the Scots say, all you need for a perfect porridge, besides the oats, is some fresh spring water, a little salt (added near the end of the cooking) and, ideally, some Scottish hill or sea air.

The porridge was once called stirabout, because it was stirred in a clockwise direction (following the course of the sun) with the right hand. Scots believe this routine ensures good luck. The porridge, bubbling in the pot, should be stirred briskly with a special wooden stick called a spurtle or sometimes a theevil or gruel-tree. If you don't have a spurtle, use a wooden spoon—never metal—and stir constantly to prevent lumps. Old-time recipes stipulate that the porridge should be cooked at least 20 minutes and mention the importance of "swelling the meal." Scots do not advocate the quick-cooking method.

The piping-hot cooked porridge is spooned into a porringer, or wooden bowl. Then each spoonful is dipped into a side dish of cold cream or milk before it is eaten. (In days past some Scotsmen preferred beer or buttermilk.) Many Highlanders believed porridge was eaten "properly" with a dram or two of whisky. The common utensil for eating porridge is a horn spoon to prevent burning the mouth.

Traditionally, porridge was eaten standing up and before the rest of the hearty breakfast. The reason is not certain. Some Scots say that it was also advisable to have one's back to the wall, for this was the only safe position for a beleaguered Highlander who feared a stab in the back from a treacherous neighbor.

Purists maintain that porridge should be eaten without any sweetening, only a pinch or two of salt. But some Scots now use sugar, honey or golden syrup.

Leftover cold cooked porridge can be sliced and topped with syrup or fried in fat and served with bacon and eggs.

Haggis

Nearly everyone seems to have heard of Scotland's controversial national dish called haggis, but few people know what it is. They just tell jokes about the mysterious creation.

Aye, so how to begin? Robbie Burns immortalized it in his satirical ode "To a Haggis" as the "great chieftan o' the puddin-race!" Comedians have described it as a "boiled bagpipe" and "giant tea bag."

Scottish postcards picture haggis as a curious short-legged Highland animal hooked on a line or in flight. "First catch your haggis," a Scot will laughingly tell you. And then there are tall tales about a beast haginasus that was hunted by the ancient Picts who used the Haggis hound to flush it from the heather.

The name gives a clue. It is thought to have derived from the Scottish word *hag*, meaning to hack, or perhaps from the French *hacher*, to chop. Haggis is actually an ancient "supersausage." It's traditionally made in a haggis bag (a sheep's paunch), which is stuffed with a mixture of chopped suet, onions, a sheep's pluck (heart, liver and lungs), oatmeal and seasonings.

'Tis a pity to have the description before the tasting. For it's the name and the ingredients of this much-maligned delicacy that puts one off. "Oh, what a glorious dish," Scots say with a twinkle in their eyes, knowing that you don't believe them.

Anyone who has not tasted haggis approaches the dish timidly. The surprise at the goodness of the fare is a great delight to Scots. I first ate haggis at the Café Royale restaurant in Edinburgh and immediately became a devotee. Later I enjoyed Yer Ain Wee Chieftain O' The Pudding Race ("the traditional haggis accompanied by neeps, tatties and ithers, and to finish a wee dram of whisky,") as an appetizer in The Four Seasons Restaurant of Glasgow's Albany Hotel. It was superb.

Now in Scotland haggis is served in various forms for breakfast, lunch and dinner but is seldom made in the home by the complicated old-fashioned process. Instead it is bought at the grocery store or butcher's shop.

Novices are advised not to undertake the making of a haggis. In America it can be purchased in cans or from some specialty food stores. In the New York City area, an excellent haggis and other Scottish specialties may be bought at two Scottish butchers: Cameron's Market, 162 Kearny Avenue, Kearny, NJ 07032, (201/991-2985); and Stewart's of Kearny, 338 Kearny Avenue, Kearny, NJ 07032, (201/991-1436). One can write to each market for a list of what's available. Kearny is a town near Newark where many Scots live and celebrate at a Scottish-American club. In the Washington, D.C. area, haggis and Scottish baked goods are available at Sharma's (Loch Lomond) Bakery and Caterers, 2500 University Blvd. East, Hyattsville, MD 20783, (301/422-6333).

While haggis is standard fare at all Scottish celebrations and is the most traditional of foods eaten in Scotland at Hogmanay (New Year's Eve), it is known in our country as the celebrated dish at the Burns Night Supper (see pages 123 and 136).

Brose

Brose is a traditional porridge soup made by pouring boiling water over oatmeal. It was the "backbone of many a sturdy Scotsman" for centuries. In the Highlands shepherds carried it in leather or wood containers to sustain them. Over the years other ingredients were added to the basic gruel. There are many variations, such as Milk Brose, Butter Brose, Blind Brose (without butter), and the famous Atholl Brose (see page 124).

Crowdie

This name was once used for all porridge-type dishes, especially those made with oatmeal and buttermilk. Crowdie has long been a breakfast dish in Scotland. Crowdie-time meant breakfast-time, or a time to eat when Robbie Burns mentioned it in "The Holy Fair."

Crowdie cream, or cranachan, is a treasured dessert (see pages 9 and 125 for recipe). A Highland dish called Cruddy Butter was made with sweet milk and butter. Ale-Crowdie, oatmeal and ale, was a popular harvest dish.

Crowdie is also the name of an ancient Highland cheese in the style of cottage cheese but smoother. In one variation, cream is added to it. Crowdie should be eaten with oatcakes and butter.

Another excellent cheese is called Caboc. It is made from double cream into little logs, which are rolled in coarse oatmeal. Galic and Hramsa are soft cream cheeses flavored with wild garlic and herbs.

In the Lowlands a soft cheese that has the Gaelic name *fuaroq* is made with milk or buttermilk and cream to which caraway seeds are sometimes added.

Fitless Cock

This is an old Highland dish made from oats, suet and onions that is shaped in the form of a cock and boiled in a cloth. It was eaten on Shrove Tuesday when cock fights were held on that day. Because fit is a foot, the name of the dish means a footless cock.

Hodgils

This is a Scottish Borders name for oatmeal dumplings. They are made with oatmeal and herbs, seasoned with salt and pepper, bound with fat, and boiled in beef broth.

Mealy Pudden

Scots enjoy black and white puddings, also called Jack and Jamie puddings. The latter is made with a sautéed mixture of oats, onions, suet and seasonings that is put into a sausage skin and boiled in broth or water. The combination called skirle, a stuffing from northeastern Scotland, is similar.

Car Cakes

These are fried pancakes made with oatmeal, milk and a leavening agent.

Sowans

This old Scottish and Irish dish was a kind of fermented porridge made with oat husks and sometimes sweetened with honey and laced with whisky. It has a curious sour taste and is a traditional Halloween dish.

Additional Traditional Foods

Here are some other dishes that do not include oats.

Flummery

This is an odd dessert or drink made in many variations, including one with oatmeal and fruits. Usually it is like a custard, flavored with honey and Scotch or nutmeg and currants.

Hattit Kit

Also called Added Kit, this is a very old Highland dish, a light pudding made by milking the cow over a bowl of warm buttermilk. The curd forms over the whey to be a "hat." Some modern versions are flavored with sugar, nutmeg and whipped cream.

Whipkull

An ancient drink, also called Whipcol, this was enjoyed in the Shetland Islands as the crowning glory of a festive breakfast on Yule, the feast of the winter solstice, on January 6. Traditionally, it was served with a large square of shortbread. A modern version is made with beaten egg yolks, sugar and rum, and sometimes whipped cream. It is served as a chilled dessert or a sauce over poached fruit.

Drinks

Scotch Whisky

This world-famous drink is a unique Scotch creation because it cannot be produced elsewhere. The secret of its special character involves the Scottish pure clear water, superb barley and peat, and even the climate.

The word whisky comes from the Gaelic *uisqebeatha* or *uisgebaugh* for "water of life." The English shortened it to whisky (spelled without an *e*).

By the 15th century the art of distilling malt was well established in the Highlands. The drink was a fierce, smoky brew that came from pot stills supervised by the head of each clan. Much of the whisky was distilled illegally, and men fought battles over the right to make the drink.

Blending of the strong Highland whisky with a milder Lowland whisky began in the 1860s. Today most Scotch whisky is a blend of the flavorful malt with a lighter cereal spirit. Pure whiskies from Scotland's individual distilleries are known as single (that is, unblended) malts. Long considered the aristocrats of Scotch, they are full-flavored, smooth and assertive—like the Scots, some say. There are traditionally four types of single malt whisky based on the four areas of Scotland where they are distilled. These are Highland malts, Lowland malts, Islay malts and Campbeltown malts.

All single malts are best drunk neat, without ice, or as they do in Scotland, with a splash of cool spring water to bring out the aroma.

"These generous whiskies, with their individual flavors, recall the world of hills and glens, of raging elements, of shelter, of divine ease," wrote Neil Gunn.

Ale

Scotland's first known alcoholic drink was a potent heather ale, made with ginger-flavored "bonny bells," or heather blossoms. In the words of Robert Louis Stevenson, it "Was sweeter far than honey, Was stronger far than wine." No exact formula for it exists.

Later, the favorite Scottish drink was ale derived from malted barley. Edinburgh and Glasgow were famous for their taverns and pie-shops where ale and pies were standard fare. Ale cups were punches made with ale and flavored with spices and aromatic herbs.

Scotland is noted for its malty ale, often dark and sometimes quite strong. Favorite brands are McEwans, Bellhaven and MacAndrews.

Drambuie

Scotland's oldest and most famous liqueur, made from Highland malt whisky, heather honey and special herbs, has a romantic history linked with a very important episode in the country's history. According to one legend, when "Bonnie Prince Charlie" came to Scotland in 1745 to try to regain the throne of his ancestors, he gave the secret formula to a close friend, Mackinnon of Skye, who sheltered him after the tragic battle of Culloden and helped him reach France safely.

The secret of the drink's preparation has remained with the Mackinnon family, who has marketed Drambuie as "Prince Charles Edward's Liqueur, A Link With the '45." The name is a contraction of the Gaelic phrase "An dram Buidheach," meaning the drink that satisfies. The Isle of Skye liqueur has a sherry-brown color showing flecks of gold in the sun, "like sunbeams imprisoned on a peat bog."

Drambuie is sold around the world.

Atholl Brose

There are many individual and regional variations for this well-known liqueur, which emerged from the Highland mists in 1475. Most are based on combining oatmeal, honey, malt whisky and sometimes thick cream.

The drink originated in Atholl, a small town in the Tayside region, and there are many stories about it. It was mentioned by Scott in his novels and Robert Louis Stevenson in *Kidnapped*. According to one legend the Duke of Atholl poured the drink into the well of his arch enemy, the Earl of Ross, who "drunk deeply of it" and thus was easily captured. It's made now to warm the festive soul on all Scottish celebrations, but especially Hogmanay. No New Year is welcomed in Scotland without it. An Atholl Brose liqueur is sold in America.

Makes about 1¼ quarts

> 1 cup water
> 1 cup honey, preferably heather
> 2½ cups Scotch whisky
> 1 cup light cream

Bring water to a boil in a large saucepan. Add honey; heat, stirring, to dissolve. Gradually add whisky; stir until combined and hot. Add cream. Remove from heat. Serve in small or thistle-shaped glasses.

Auld Man's Milk

A morning drink or pick-me-up, this is made by combining cream, sugar and egg yolks to which whisky and beaten egg whites are added. Served in a punch bowl or glasses, it is topped with grated nutmeg.

Glasgow Punch

This mixture of sugar, lemon or lime juice, rum and spring water was once popular in Glasgow clubs and is still served as a traditional drink. Sometimes it is made with brandy instead of rum.

Glayva

A modern Scotch liqueur, it is made with whisky, spices and aromatic herbs.

Glen Mist

A dryish Scotch liqueur blended with herbs, honey, spices and fine, fully matured whisky. It is sold in America.

Het Pint

Until modern times the great Hogmanay drink was Het Pint or hot ale, spiced and laced with whisky. It was carried through city streets in copper or toddy kettles shortly before midnight and passed in cupfuls so everyone could toast "a gude New Year to one and all, and mony may ye see." Flavored with sugar and frothy with whipped eggs, it is served very hot in mugs.

Makes about 2½ quarts

> 2 quarts ale
> 1 teaspoon freshly grated nutmeg
> ½ cup sugar
> 3 large eggs
> 1 cup Scotch whisky

Heat ale and nutmeg in a kettle until hot; do not boil. Add sugar; leave until dissolved. Beat eggs in a small bowl; add ¾ cup hot ale mixture; beat to blend well. Pour into hot ale mixture, stirring while adding. Reheat until hot; beat again. Serve at once in mugs.

Pirr

This Shetland Island hot drink, made by mixing oatmeal, brown sugar, cream of tartar and milk into a paste to which boiling water is added, was esteemed as a cure for colds when taken before going to bed.

Posset

This was an ale or wine-milk drink, spiced and thickened with oatmeal.

Shandy

A shandy or shandy gaff is a refreshing long drink made of beer or ale mixed with ginger beer, ginger ale or lemonade. The origin of the name is unknown. Shandies were first introduced as a source of vitamin C for sailors. Now they are popular pub drinks. Commercial versions are sold in America.

Toddy

A toddy, or whisky-toddy, is a traditional hot drink made with sugar or honey, boiling water and Scotch. It is sipped with slow and loving care as a drink and taken as a cure for colds and as an elixir of life.

Scottish Holidays

Scots have a flair for celebrating their treasured holidays. They show respect for their heritage and ancient traditions in many ways, but especially with a festive meal. A gathering of the clans, whether small or large, is a spirited event with a "thumping good supply" of favorite foods and a great deal of sentiment expressed with toasts.

Drink is an important element of Scottish banquets, and the *quaich,* a drinking cup, is filled generously and often. Of Highland origin, the name derives from the Gaelic *cuach,* a cup. It is wide and shallow, with wedge-shaped handles, easy to pass as a loving cup. Usually made of wood, there are also pewter and silver cups.

There is a Scottish saying, "Moderation, Sir, aye, moderation is my motto. Nine or ten is reasonable refreshment, but after that it is apt to degenerate into drinking." The Scots are notorious hard drinkers. They like to have a good time and enjoy the "social glass," as Burns called it. There are many drinking songs and poems. A famous one by Sir Harry Lauder was about a nostalgic farewell libation or "Just a wee deoch-an-dorris, Before we gang awa." Another, called 'A braw Scots nicht' by Will Ogilvie, goes: "When the last big bottle's empty and dawn creeps grey and cold, And the last clan-tartan's folded and the last damned lie is told; When they totter down the footpaths in a braw unbroken line,

To peril of the passers and the tune of 'Auld Lang Syne; You can tell the folk at breakfast as you watch the fearsome sicht, They've only been assisting at a braw Scots Nicht!".

Burns Night

Throughout the world Robbie Burns's admirers don the tartan to honor the life and work of Scotland's beloved poet-hero on the anniversary of his birth, January 25. He died in 1796, and Burns clubs began as early as 1801.

'Tis a jolly gathering of nostalgic Scots, dressed in their finest, who sit down at tables for the legendary Burns Night supper, a serious literary event as well as a ceremonial meal. First there is whisky. And then the prayer, known as the Selkirk Grace, about "being poor, honest and happy." It was repeated by Burns when dining with the Earl of Selkirk. "Some hae meat and canna eat, And some wad eat that want it; But we hae meat and we can eat, And sae the Lord be thankit. . ."

The meal begins with soup, Scotch Broth or Cock-A-Leekie, accompanied by whisky. Then, to the skirl of bagpipes, applause and cry of "Hail Great Chieftain," the haggis on a silver platter arrives. Someone recites Burns's famous ode, "To A Haggis," and everyone joins in a Gaelic toast, *slainte,* or good health, to the hot and spicy haggis, drenched with whisky, that is ceremoniously cut with a *skein dhu,* a dirk (short straight dagger worn in the stocking). It is served regally with "neeps an' tatties" (mashed turnips and potatoes) and "wee nips" of whisky.

As the evening warms up, there is singing of Burns's songs, followed by a principal Burns speech, the "Immortal Memory," an improvised oration, both serious and humorous, given by a distinguished guest.

After a rich dessert, such as Tipsy Laird or cranachan, shortbreads, cakes and, perhaps, cheese, there follow more heartfelt toasts, piping and spirited dancing. The celebrating goes on until the wee hours of the morning, ending with a rendition of "Auld Lang Syne," Burns's best-known song.

Can there be any doubt about the sturdiness of the Scots?

St. Andrew's Night

Saint Andrew is regarded as the patron saint of Scotland. He looks after all Scots at home and abroad. Scots celebrate the apostle's feast day, November 30, with a festival that may be a St. Andrew's Society Ball (as in Washington, D.C.) or an elaborate dinner (as with the Saint Andrew's Society of the State of New York).

Saint Andrew of Scotland is mentioned in the Bible as a fisherman, the brother of Simon called Peter. According to legend, a Greek monk named St. Regulus (or Rule) was divinely inspired to steal St. Andrew's relics and take them on a journey. Led by dreams, he ended up shipwrecked on the North Sea coast of Fife near what is now the lovely old Royal Burgh of St. Andrews, the capital of the golfing world. It was here that he converted the Picts to Christianity, goes the story.

St. Andrew societies were founded to give aid to Scots in many American centers quite early in the 18th century. Among the first were those of Charleston, S.C., Alexandria, Va., Philadelphia and New York. Later they became prominent charitable organizations, and the male members liked to gather for good food and drink, especially on the Saint's feast day.

Any of the dinners feature a traditional Scottish menu, recitations such as Burns's "The Land O' Cakes" (originally oatcakes), and lots of convivial drinking.

In London a popular drink for the occasion is a Rob Roy made with half Scotch whisky, half sweet vermouth, and two dashes of Angostura Bitters.

Hogmanay

New Year's Eve, Hogmanay, is a merry gathering of family and friends to celebrate with traditional customs and good fare.

The word is thought to have derived from the old French *hoguignane,* meaning the last day of the year. In Scottish towns the evening once began with gatherings to "burn out" the evils of the Old Year with bonfires, singing and the drinking of Het Pint (see page 132 for recipe).

In the homes, preparations are readied for parties with groaning boards of haggis, cold salmon, pork and lamb pies, cold or hot game dishes, smoked fish, an array of breads, oatcakes, shortbreads, spice and fruit cakes, cream desserts, and the traditional Black Bun (see pages 89 and 90), as well as an assortment of drinks.

After the stroke of midnight the first-footing ceremony commences. Of utmost importance is the arrival of the first person to cross the threshold. For, according to tradition, this determines the fortunes of the household for the year to come. With luck, it will be a tall, dark-haired man said to be a sign of good fortune.

The welcome first-footer, and later the guests, bring handsel (good luck) gifts symbolizing life, hospitality and warmth, such as cheese (magic), bread, cake, a lump of coal to place on the fire, red herring (plenty) and, always, whisky.

Then the celebrating and feasting begin, often lasting until dawn. No Scottish New Year can be welcomed without a drink of Atholl Brose and the singing of "Auld Lang Syne" with its toast to absent friends and days of long ago.

Many customs from Scotland became popular in colonial American communities, particularly those of the Mid-Atlantic region like Alexandria, Va., where they have been observed since the city's founding by Alexander Ramsey. Citizens of this old port love to celebrate their Scottish heritage with a number of year-round events.

The holiday season begins in early December with an annual Christmas Walk. *Ceud Mile Failte,* A Hundred Thousand Welcomes, rings through Old Town Alexandria with a colorful parade, Scottish dancing and bagpiping, choral groups, visits to historic homes, and Advent services. For years a special Hogmanay observation was held with a public reception at The Carlyle House, built in 1752 and patterned after a Scottish country manor. The ceremony of "first-footing" was held on the House's terrace.

Now Hogmanay is celebrated in many private homes and in Old Town public eating places where the city's kilted Pipes and Drums drop by to perform. Always ready for their visits is James Graham, a native of Glasgow, chef and co-owner of Scotland Yard, a restaurant specializing in Scottish cuisine. He greets one and all in full regalia.

According to Graham, Hogmanay is more than just a holiday. "The superstition is that the way you are at the beginning of the year is the way you'll be the rest of the year. There are no enemies that night. Everyone makes up, even if they don't get along all the rest of the year."

As for food, he describes that as a "table loaded with a great number and variety of dishes. But the one thing that's in place is shortbread. Everyone has shortbread. No one has no shortbread. It's the traditional dish."

The Scottish spirit of conviviality lives on— not only in Alexandria but wherever Scots are.

An Acknowledgment

Early in the 19th century there was a notable renaissance in Edinburgh and the Lowlands of ancient Scots dishes and customs. Sir Walter Scott, "the whole world's darling," who had a keen interest in his country's food and traditions, did a great deal to foster and promote the revival of Scottish self-awareness.

Scott is thought to have been instrumental in the publication of one of Scotland's most important culinary works, *The Cook and Housewife's Manual,* or *Meg Dods' Cookery,* as it was commonly known. It was published in Edinburgh in 1826 under the pseudonym of Mistress Margaret Dods.

This name was taken from that of Scott's eccentric innkeeper character in his novel of social life, *St. Ronan's Well.* In it she runs the Cleikum Club, which serves high quality food and drink.

The *Manual* was actually compiled and written by Mrs. Isobel Christian Johnstone, an author of some note and wife of an Edinburgh publisher. The humorous introduction, a dialogue between gastronomes who plan the Club, is so clever that it is thought to have been written by Scott. Whether or not he was the author remains a mystery. But the book has much literary merit and is valuable for its collection of historic recipes.

Later, in *The Scots Kitchen* (1929) F. Marian McNeil includes many excerpts from Dods's *Manual* and Scott's novels, as well as a unique collection of recipes culled from old Scottish books and enlivened by the author's authoritative remarks.

All modern Scottish cookbooks, including this one, have adapted many of the dishes of these early authors and owe them a debt of gratitude. Thanks to them all.

Index

141

143